One Last Call

A GUIDE
FOR THE
ACHIEVEMENT
OF
LASTING PEACE

by Donnell L. Harris

Prescott **P**ress, **I**nc.

Prescott Press, Inc.
P.O. Box 53788
Lafayette, Louisiana 70505

Library of Congress
Card Catalog Number 98-66876
ISBN 0-933451-39-3

Will,
I've meet many guys but, none like you. Thanks for being some one I could be proud of. Good luck.

8/20/98

Thank You

Mom & Dad

Granddaddy

Mr. & Mrs. James Walker

Dr. & Mrs. E. E. Cleveland

Mark & Kathy

&

a special thanks to

my girlfriend and wife, Liz,

without her hard work and determination

you probably wouldn't be reading this

One Last Call

Dedication

The pages of this project are dedicated first to God. With wondrous anticipation, it is those who believe in Him who find hope. Surely it is God alone, our Supreme Providence, who, even in the company of those who despise us, prepares a table of abundance. By His hands we are filled with food, even to spare. When I am hungry, I can go to Him in faith, knowing that just by the opening of His hands, He gives satisfaction to everything that lives.

Secondly, I dedicate this work to the citizens of Oklahoma City, Oklahoma. On April 19, 1995, our nation was stunned and taught a severe lesson in trust. As a national body, we learned that it is not other people we should fear so much as those who are misguided and evil. The villains, who stole the headlines that day, were deluded cowards whose limited minds were deceived into choosing conflict over constructive measures in the quest for peace. The residents of Oklahoma City struggled with the deeds of evil. They fought back the forces of conflict with the weapons of courage, faith, hope, and goodwill.

We saw, in their faces, reflections of our faces. The slain, the injured, and those survivors racked with pain, mirrored us all. They represented the races, sexes, ages, religions, and socio-political diversities of earth. They displayed the beauty of the American quilt, the flavor of the American stew, and they worked together, as a positive blend in the melting pot. As the quilt, they represented the pulchritudinous fabric of patches tied together by the common thread of community, neighbor helping neighbor. The mixtures, represented by the stew and melting pot, poured out individual stories of love and life. Some of the stories were of reunification, as love lost became love found, restored, and renewed. Some of the stories of life were stories of hope challenged by trial, conflict, and obstacle. Here, seen as one, were faces of wealth and poverty. People educated in some great colleges and universities, along with others whose lessons were learned from the experiences and challenges presented by life, were working together and suffering together, as one.

In unison, God heard our soulful chorus of prayers. These prayers were lifted by voices representing all religious backgrounds, faiths, and leanings. On April 19, the powers of good were braved, barraged, and battled by evil. On April 20, newspapers the world over headlined, "GOOD HAD THE VICTORY," thanks to the actions of a residentially fragmented family united by catastrophe in a mission of hope and help.

We must not forget the children in the daycare center. We must not forget the workers who reported to this federal building for work, day after day. We must never forget the citizens who entered the building for assistance. We cannot allow the slain to have died in vain. If we forget the lessons of that tragic day, the faces of grief and pain, the surviving mothers, fathers, children, brothers or sisters, or if we ignore the hurt felt by grandparents and grandchildren, or the grief of aunts, uncles, friends, and lovers, we are cursed to witness repeated acts of mindless terror and destruction.

We must remember those slaughtered, but also are challenged to keep in our prayers, as long as we breathe, a prayer for the survivors. Join me in praying for them that each day in the future becomes a gift of love, hope, and good will.

To the governor and citizens Oklahoma, especially the residents of Oklahoma City, and its vicinity: May God continually bless you all by unfolding from your tragedies triumphs. May you all be showered by the good fortune of life, liberty, and happiness, now and always.

Contents

ix

Introduction

There are some who believe that we are the progenitors of beings evolved and developed from a simple one-cell existence. There are others who believe we are the generations of children descended from Adam and Eve. Some believe that we, like Adam and Eve, were molded by the hand of God. Others simply do not care. To them, the questions concerning our existence pale and are overshadowed by questions of personal survival. From whatever standpoint, we all will agree that humankind was destitute long before we knew what destitution was.

Let's face it, whether by developing from an amoeboid state or a supremely intellectual state, when humans developed, material resources and possessions were not there. Creativity was, as it is now, the only chance for survival. During the last two centuries, we have moved, by our creativity, from farm to factory. Our vision, met with creativity and action, caused the industrial revolution. At the beginning of the twentieth century, we moved humanity from ground to air. By the end of the century, air included the reaches of outer space.

Spanning my grandfather's lifetime alone, we may examine the reaches of the twentieth century. Granddaddy was born on July 4, 1901. During his lifetime, he witnessed growth. This growth was human as much as technological. He saw the horse and buggy transform rapidly into automobiles. These automobiles, trailed by a cloud of dust, sped into an aerospace age when humans were lifted to travel over the rainbow and beyond the clouds, then to the stars. In his lifetime alone, my granddad witnessed the evolution of humanity in every imaginable way. He witnessed great strides in education, industry, and technology, but, in one area, his eyes were met with disappointment.

Nature, at conception, placed his hands upon a door knob. At birth, the turn was made. The door leading into the corridors of time slowly creaked open revealing wonders. Like Granddad, everyone has turned that door handle. The advance was a completed first step on a new history. Each step we make becomes a foot print which the followers, into and beyond the twenty-first century, will follow.

Having tied up our transactions in the twentieth century, we follow forerunners such as teachers, inventors, businessmen, writers, ministers, statesmen, and peace-keepers who, with positive vision, have already led the way to an excitingly new and challenging future. Sadly, however, some of our brothers and sisters have allowed themselves to march into the twenty-first century behind crude, selfish, cynical men. Some would follow hoggishly proud, self-centered, self-indulgent, self-interested, self-seeking, and self-pleasing men whose foul breath and grinning lips drip constantly with lies. Without moral conviction, these men are responsible for the bloodletting of the innocent.

Foolishly, many have paraded behind drummers who pound out a rhythm of wicked schemes as they march from one evil deed to another. With spiritual anguish, many well-intentioned but misguided followers have booted along behind self-established leaders who claim to forge out a trail of peace along the path of brotherhood, while stirring dissension. They have created sour notes, within the harmony of the human family. For this reason, I give, "One Last Call."

The chief goal of these pages is to present a challenge, first to the American family, then to the world. Although we are under no current threat of nuclear extermination, we advance unwittingly on the path to self-annihilation. By this I mean that the human spirit will die, smothered by the loss of interest in life and the bounties of joy it brings. We are challenged to lead this world in the redevelopment of community. Those of us who have Islamic, Judaic, and Christian leanings are near-neighbors, living in separate mental homes, yet bonded in the neighborhood of God. Knowing this creates cooperative personhood. It further promotes people of good will, who understand, to lead in the development of a fairer society. On this premise, I give, "One Last Call."

"One Last Call" is a challenge for every person, without, regardless of station in life, to join the author in an ongoing venture ridding this world of the evils of intolerance, bigotry, and hatred. The shackles of prejudice are decisive. Racism, sexism, disrespect for religious freedom, political affiliations, national origins, or choices of private concern, carry no positive energy. Waging war against these evils will reconstitute hope and lasting peace. The plan is simple. It only requires an answer of "Yes, I will help." This will make the reader part of the solution. Anyone part of the solution will not be part of the problem. For this reason, I offer, "One Last Call."

By challenging the American family first, is the author guilty of some form of imperialistic bigotry? Is his belief that only Americans can lead such a venture? By all means, no! It is only that he has realized the United States of America, while constantly voicing peace and democracy abroad, by seeking treaties and accords, announcing efforts to foster peace and brotherhood among nations, has moved very slowly and inattentively on its own problems of unification. Constant and willful intolerance has poisoned its waters. Racism and sexism are its main pollutants. "Charity begins at home," and the American family must heed the call. To this end, I make, "One Last Call."

America has been described in many positive ways. It has been called the great melting pot. It has been held up as a quilt and compared with a stew. Each of these descriptive designations holds steadfast a firm belief, no matter how hypocritical, in the American ideal. This ideal is buried deep and held securely in documents supporting its sovereignty. It resonates in the Declaration of Independence: "We hold these truths to be self-evident, that all Men are created equal," and "that they are endowed by their Creator with certain inalienable rights that among these are life, liberty and the pursuit of happiness." The Preamble of the Constitution voices the establishment of justice, the domestic tranquillity, general welfare, and the blessings of liberty. What other nation boasts a Bill of Rights which guarantees the non-abridgement of the rights of free speech, privacy, and countless other (Amendment #9, U.S. Constitution). But the American house is not clean. The American home has been defiled by the disease of prejudice. Its heart, though good, lays lifeless on the world stage, attacked by a willful avoidance of the nutrients of love and respect. So first, to America, I sound, "One Last Call."

The world must understand its attachment to and understanding of positive descriptions of the American home. First, the melting pot. America as a melting pot evokes the image of people of all backgrounds brought together in a great pot or a crucible of some sort, and melted together to create a beautiful mixture for the mold of brotherhood. Somehow the gaffers of the American psyche stole this meaning. They have set out, all under a so-called conservative voice, to destroy this view. They have done this by pandering to racism. This was strategically completed by warnings of miscegeny and destructive images of amalgamation. Social and cultural assimilation were clouded by negativity. The pure meaning of the term of the "melting pot" is embodied in the extraordinary introduction to the constitution: "We The People."

America has also been defined as a quilt; many cold nights were unnoticed thanks to the comfort of a quilt. Some quilts were tattered and torn giving face to age holding memories of time. Other quilts were works of art. Ornate or nostalgic pieces of commemorative patchwork were tied together by common thread. The American quilt has been held high, boasting its beauties. The beauties include our unique differences that create a pattern of unmatched design. Although we differ by race, age, tongue, sex, religious affiliation, and political leanings, we could speak of our commonality as "The American Family."

America has been compared to a stew not only aromatic while cooking, but delicious and healthful. The major ingredients of a good stew, the potatoes, onions, carrots, peas, and meat, maintain identity yet promote the taste of union. The common element here is culture. By design, the American scene is rich and flavorful with an incredibly seasoned and diverse culture. Every crack and crevice of human diversity is found on the national front. America, as no other nation, has a prize winning recipe for appetizing unification.

In America, the melting pot, quilt, and stew, one often hears the term, "the good ol' days." Depending on era, what was good for some was not good for all. Take, for example, the days of the American frontier and the arrival of settlers pillaging the national wealth and beauty which belonged to the native Americans. Take the American Revolutionary War and the lives it claimed in the construction of a Republic. Take the darkest hours of exploitation by the evil institution of slavery, the disunion of a nation, a civil war in which brother killed brother. Take the U.S. involvement in World War I, the Great Depression, World War II, the Korean Conflict, the bloody struggle for Civil Rights, the Vietnam War and the Watergate scandal. The "good ol' days," for the most part, never existed. Songwriter, Billy Joel best said it: "the good ol' days weren't always good and tomorrow ain't as bad as it seems." Every period of time was fraught with trauma. These traumas, no matter how relative, no matter how small, seemed insurmountable to those who lived through them.

These pages only look backward to take inventory. They serve as an aid to rid us of the baggage that would hinder peace for all peoples. *One Last Call* highlights the beauties of a place we call home. *One Last Call* is a summons to alter our direction as a nation and a world. *One Last Call* is a challenge to cooperation, by the evocation of love and respect for all humankind. *One Last Call* will begin a movement for men and women of this world to join in a spirit of brotherhood and sisterhood and the establishment of peace. The words in this book can only serve as an aid in construction of a rational policy. It should be understood that no national policy or world policy can survive without private citizens making a commitment. To be a viable policy, the agreements for peace must be fair and equal for all.

Read this book. It does not contain all the answers, however, it promotes an intelligent start and a great beginning for all people of this world in their movement into and beyond the twenty-first century. This is *One Last Call.*

1

Turn the Tides

Thinking back on my childhood, I realize romance was no stranger. There were three girls for whom I felt great admiration. First, there was Cathy, nicknamed "Butterball" by her grandfather. He called me "Sarge." Perhaps it had something to do with the little green shirt I often wore. It had a patch which was sewn on the chest that read "US Army." It also had striped patches on the sleeves, just below the shoulder. Cathy and her grandfather lived next door. She and I were about the same age. Together, we would run to catch the school bus. It was not because the bus needed capturing, but often Mr. Sandman granted us a late release.

During those years, I don't ever recall that Cathy and I were in the same class. I do, however, remember the evenings and weekends we shared when school was out. We were so close. I don't remember when, but I do know how we fell apart. We both grew up. She is still a friend. Now and then I see her. Here and there I get in a few words: "Hey," "Hello," "How are ya doing," "So what's going on." I guess time created some strange distance. It is now a distance that leaves us worlds apart.

Then there was Norma Lee. She was Lorraine's daughter. I met her and her mother through Norma's grandmother, Vi, short for Violet. She was a member of my church. Norma Lee, with her sisters Gloria and Sheila, lived in some faraway place called California.

Because I lived in Maryland, Norma Lee's her California home was as distant as the moon, just not as extreme. From time to time Norma and her family would visit and stay with Vi. One summer they stayed at my home. Even with this, distance would come between us again, and all admiration would be reduced to that "girl who lived out there."

But it was not distance that would steal my third friend. She and I met in the first grade. She knocked me off my feet. If there could have ever been a puppy love, it was for her. Gail was her name. She was a little pudgy and cute as a button. This freckle-faced little girl was a peach who, for the rest of her days at the elementary school, would find my devoted friendship. Being convinced and convicted, I look back believing, that if it was God planting angels in little people, He created an angelic home in her. I found comfort being around her as well as her brother, Wayne. They were my friends.

Our teacher was Mrs. Ethel Mae Thompson. She was one of the last links in a great succession of educators. Because she taught my older brother and sisters, she seemed older than time. She also seemed wiser than Solomon. Most of the kids at my school feared her. Horror story after horror story would fill the air about her treatment of pupils who were "bad." This fear, no doubt, was worse than being sent to Hell.

I didn't fear Mrs. Thompson. She couldn't have been that bad. She never harmed my oldest brother and she surely did not snuff-out my sister, Jackie, who I'm quite certain gave her a good share of challenges. She also knew my parents. She even knew my granddaddy, Jack. Seemingly everybody knew him. He was the man who raised sweet potato plants. His real name was Emory Harris; I never knew why they called him Jack.

Mrs. Thompson loved my family. Sometimes I would sit back and look at her. Seeing beyond her famous wig and glasses perched on her nose, her eyes, smiled. Her smile radiated love for all of us. Her special love would give us hope. Sitting in her classes, I learned no dream would be too hard to catch and no challenge too big to overcome.

Each day, Mrs. Thompson would begin our class by calling on us to share current events from the newspaper. We would listen attentively knowing we would be quizzed later. One day Leslie read an article about the Baltimore Orioles. Upon completion, the teacher would ask who could recite the members of the team. Tom's hand went up. He was called on. Without stuttering, he called out every member of the team in the order of the article. He did not hesitate or pause. He even called out Andy Etchebarren. Then we would sing. Mrs. Thompson would call on us to lead some sort of song service.

One song that she taught us is the embodiment of this book. I wanted no one to lead us in singing this song except Gail. It said:

> The more we get together,
> together, together,
> The more we get together,
> The happier we would be.
> For my friends are your friends,
> And your friends are my friends.
> The more we get together,
> The happier we would be.

With excitement, Gail would lead us in that song. She did it so beautifully that it still sounds in my heart today.

I never understood time. It never stops. Time brought an end to the fourth grade. Bussing and relocating had taken my friend Gail. At home was still Cathy and a host of other community friends. But when I entered the fifth grade, there was no Wayne and definitely no Gail. Her memories were beyond the windows. It was a disappointment lifted away and carried by the wind.

Elementary school was a unique time in life. Not until those poor, but richly dressed, people from the new developments would come, would I know anything about race-consciousness and an ongoing struggle for territory. I would have never understood "the man." I would not have heard in the exchange of name calling the most painful word, "nigger." I never noticed a "Black b——" until I heard the epithet as an insult. Somehow, it all related to those angry people I saw on television. Everybody was scattered, trying to get something. "The man" was holding it. He was playing some sophisticated game of "keep away."

I was drafted into a social war. It was a war of race. Kids whom I once admired were now lining up on the other side. The crucible we called the melting pot had overheated and was about to explode. This was evident when I got to sixth grade.

For sixth grade, I attended a private Christian Academy. It was operated by the Seventh-Day Adventists. Although the school boasted its Christian education, little was done to rid it of its racial disunity and willful participation in bigotry. I never found the pressure of being different so annoying as my days there. The worst part was that the principal, faculty, and staff had no understanding, not even a clue, of the effects of prejudice.

Even there I found friendships. One such friend was Mark, nicknamed "Tater." He was in my class. He, his brother, and sister, were kind to me. I remember once going on a field trip to Harper's Ferry, West Virginia. I would not have attended if his family had not opened its doors and welcomed me into their home to stay overnight. Some students did not appreciate that. For some strange reason , Mark too was usually slighted. Perhaps his ancestry was not always welcomed either.

Trouble after trouble, trial after trial occurred. Pain after pain would be absorbed. My two brothers who attended with me would be scarred for life. How unfair . . . how unfair! There was only one way to hold on. I was challenged to network my friendships with persons of tolerance. Teachers and students who granted comfort and welcome would never know how many mental wounds were bandaged by their love and respect. I constantly protested my parents sending us to this cesspool of White dominance. The majority of the 7th Day Adventists were clueless. How embarrassing that they identified themselves with the family of Christ.

On one of the worst days, I was accused of writing a curse word in my textbook. The student who did this in view of me promptly and hypocritically, with an angelic charm, raised his hand. "Miss Neidemeier," he said summoning the attention of the teacher. "Lewis," as they called me, since my first name was too ethnic, "wrote a swear word in his book."

The class gasped. Some even claimed to have seen me do it. Of course, if I was accused it had to be true. This was an early lesson in the American way.

Miss Neidemeier questioned me; I was told to admit to the wrong doing or accept punishment. No punishment would ever pain as much as the situation of vulnerability as I was in. I accepted the punishment. Before the class, I was shamed. The teacher shredded a bar of Ivory soap and forced me to put it in my mouth. She then escorted me to the water fountain just outside the classroom to fill the remaining areas of my mouth with water. I was then lead back to stand before the class. I was told not to swallow or spit out this bubbling mixture. I would remain this way until I was willing to confess I had committed this deed. I remained on my feet asthmatically finding it difficult to breath. However, I would remain firm in my resolve not to admit to this charge that was untrue.

It was lunch time. "Lewis," she asked, "are you ready to tell the truth?" I nodded. "You will admit that you wrote this?" she questioned. My answer was no. My eyes were now weighted with tears. I was hurt. How could a human, a child of God, a member of Christ's family be so abused?

In hers eyes, I read perplexity. She saw in me a stubbornness that would be my hallmark in life. She realized that her determination to bring on a confession was no match to my determination to tell the truth. A strategic blow had been planted in her heart. She was in retreat. She allowed me to empty this soapy gruel from my mouth. "Lewis, did you write this?"

With red stained and tear-filled eyes I cried. "No!"

She invited me and the accusing student to her desk. We were instructed to stay behind, missing lunch until we agreed to tell the truth. His evil deed was no match for his appetite. He begged me to say that I did it. I asked him why. What would cause him to do this? It was not funny and certainly not nice. However, I assured him of the fact that I still loved him. This was my duty. No matter how challenged in life, a true child of God must find and keep a commitment to love. Commitment to love brings peace.

Tears filled his eyes as he confessed to me his sorrow. After pleading and begging me to admit that I wrote the swear word, he agreed to confess. I told him it was not necessary. He said he knew, but he was hungry. I guess my determination somehow caused me to miss out on the smell of hot Italian spiced spaghetti being served with garlic bread in the cafeteria for lunch.

We went to the cafeteria. "Miss Neidemeier," I called out to the teacher. "He wants to tell you something."

"Miss Neidemeier," he quiveringly said. "Don't be mad at me. I wrote those words in Lewis' book."

Her expression betrayed no surprise. It was I who would be the recipient of the surprise to come. She told him lunch was over but he could go out for recess.

Wow! No punishment? I had again been wounded. I was knocked down. My heart was bleeding, gushing innocent blood. There was no justice. This was most unfair. I learned double standards at a very young age. This was and would remain my best example.

Maintaining a thread of composure, I started for the door. "Lewis" she called, "come back."

"But he said that he did it," I protested to Miss Neidemeier.

"I know," she replied.

"Why didn't you punish him?" I asked.

"Lewis, sit down. Lewis you did a good thing."

Now either this was my first megadose of confusion, or this red-headed, freckled-faced beauty was losing her mind. "Lewis, look at you," she went on to say. "His life will be easy. You are going to be challenged. People will accuse you of wrong things and they will always believe in your capacity to do them. What you did was right. No matter what is done to you, even if people threaten to kill you, stand up for what is right."

Those words, that advice, was surgically and permanently attached to my brain. It made me what I am. That teacher, who I thought lost her mind that day, having previously been a friendly ally of hope and a bastion of protection for me, had given me a gift. It was a gift that no one, not even the richest of men, having been taught in the most prestigious institutions would ever give me. She shared the recipe of trust. She paid my tuition, granting me entry to the school of integrity.

I left that school, my parents giving in to my pleas. Not only for me but my brothers as well. I left that year having earned the prize of wisdom. I do not know for sure whether it was for peace of mind or piece of money that my parents returned us to the public school system. I was just happy to be back. Nothing had changed. If the race problem had changed, it was only for the worse. White race baiters would urge battles. Blacks with blood boiling, resenting an exaggerated treatment of racism, were ready, willing, and able for battle. It was the lowest common denominator of two groups labeled "rednecks" and "niggers" that would cause the more intelligent, more tolerant keepers of peace to draw an imaginary line. This line successfully established limits for interaction. No doubt parents and guardians, having themselves bowed to this subtle form of racism, passively but strongly encouraged it.

One day during my senior year of high school, I was walking on the sidewalk about to enter the school. I looked up, and standing against the wall was my old pal, Gail. My eyes looked deep into her. I wondered whether she remembered me. With a strange expression of grief on her face, she waved. I, having bowed foolishly to that imaginary line of social interaction, walked away without speaking. My heart throbbed with desire to say hello. I wanted to ask how she and Wayne were getting along. I still thought she was beautiful. I was weak. The disease of racial intolerance had displayed its symptoms in me. Was there a cure? Is there a remedy?

One week later, in my final weeks of high school, I sat at my desk. The morning announcements were coming over the public address system. We lacked attention. When the pledge of allegiance was said, I stood by apathetically. At the end of the announcements, a hush fell over our conversations. We were asked to be silent in memory of a classmate. My heart would die as I learned of the death of my old school pal, Gail, by her own hands, with a pull of a trigger. She had committed suicide. My friend's life had been shattered by an extremely judgmental and ignorant society of disunity.

Gail's life was destroyed. A promise was shattered. What guilt! In her face, I witnessed the surge. I saw the waters drowning her hopes. I did nothing. My diseased, weakened mind had barred me from tossing out a lifeline. Was it I? Could I have turned back the tide?

2

Better Days Are Coming

Morning was in full swing. Rush hour traffic had begun to flow. Steadily the flow increased. Quickly the increase caused its daily gridlock. Workers were laboring, preparing a stage on the parking lot near the busiest intersection in town. It was the day he would come to town. Everyone was excited; we all had the idea he would be our next President.

Over the noise of engines were horns and the occasional wail of a siren. More and more attention was taken from the roadway and surrendered to the flags and posters that seemingly sprouted up in this political garden. Now and then you would hear the metallic squealing of brakes and burning tires from drivers' slamming on their brakes.

It was hard to believe he was coming here. We were not fast like New York City, or big like L.A. or Chicago. Most big-name politicians had passed us by. However, reality was presenting itself a little more heartfelt. I watched police and men in black suits with dark sunglasses pace over the area with dogs. Yellow warning banners were put in place, roping off restricted areas. They even had a couple of those scanners like the ones at airports checking for weapons.

The crowd began to swell. There were stragglers here and there. Later there was an army of people. I saw a couple of local ministers. They always seemed attracted to events like this. I saw my barber and a few teachers I had back in grade school. Just below the platform, a band had gathered and

were playing patriotic songs. Red, white and blue were everywhere. In the streamers, in the balloons which were later
launched. Never had so much excitement filled the air as the
excitement of this crowd awaiting his eminent arrival.

Noon arrived. The lunchtime crowd had been pouring in
since 11:30. He was fifteen minutes late. Speechmaker after
speechmaker from the podium would insight the crowd to
waves and cheers. Posters held by supporters would seemingly
leap up and down as they danced among the audience. By
12:30, chanting was at its peak.

Horns began to blow and sirens were blaring. From a
distance, flashing lights appeared. His bus had finally arrived.
As the bus bearing his name boldly plastered on the side
entered the parking lot, the speaker announced, "He is here!"
Cheers filled the air, eyes widened as the hungry mob strained
against the barricades. As he moved from the bus, he was met
by a sea of microphones. Cameramen were scowling, lights
were flashing to get that perfect photo. First, he shook hands
with the governor, then the county executive, and mayor. He
was joined by a hungry throng of worshippers, as he made his
way to the podium. The crowd grew silent as the announcement was made: "I give you the next President of the United
States." An orgasmic cheer erupted. Applause again had filled
the air as he made his way to the mike.

After a few typically funny, politically satirical jokes, he
went on to ask for our votes. America needed us, we were
told. We needed each other. He promised that tomorrow
would be a new day. Most of the speech went unremembered.
Basically, he said no more than any other politician.

How disappointing. My mind echoes his themes. He
started by saying, "My friends, awake from your slumber. My
fellow Americans, vote for me." I believe he was telling us he
had the answers to every problem. People wear crucifixes in
memory of the last person who could substantiate that claim.
This guy had no robe, he wore no sandals. However, he
thought he could fix it all, or maybe he just wanted us to
believe he could.

The crowd cheered as he danced from issue to issue. In a shallow way this highly visible, well-dressed, aristocrat would prostitute himself, spitting out highly polished lines that any well-trained performer could give, even under a tent owned by Ringling Brothers. Yes, he claimed conservatism. Hissing like a snake, he called for unity. He threw out boast after boast, brag after brag, for nearly an half hour. The only breaths he took were during applause. Last time I remember seeing an act like this was with the trained seals at the aquarium.

He claimed that he could solve our many problems, he would fight to lower our taxes. He told us our children were stupid and our teachers could not teach. He let us know our streets were plagued with violence and our prisons were over-crowded. The penal systems were constantly placing danger-ous men on the streets. I was beginning to wonder who al-lowed him to roam free. Children could not pray in schools. Every woman was getting an abortion. He aligned himself with the flag and told us how proud he was to be an Ameri-can. I got the impression he wanted to lead what he believed to be the worst nation on the face of the Earth. Although America has a lot of problems, it has a lot of great things going for it. How low would a man reach to feed his ego?

Our nation was unsafe, but according to whose perspec-tive? I don't think it ever was. Back when the Native Ameri-cans owned the land, this had been an unsafe frontier. Greedy men raped and pillaged as they climbed to the top of some hill. When was this nation safe? Perhaps it was when America boasted its own system of apartheid. Was it when most blacks had employment under the evil institution of slavery? Maybe it was during World War II, when many Japanese Americans were imprisoned in internment camps. Perhaps, it was when Catholics were seen as devils paying homage to an antichrist. Perhaps, it is now as women, blacks, the disabled, and people with alternative lifestyles fight for equal rights.

The ghost of civil rights promoters, the spirit of the slain Kent State students, and the souls of many workers befriend-ing peace whose lives were extinguished because of their in-sistence that America live up to its creed, cry in unison from their graves. The land is not safe! It has not been safe, is not safe and will not be safe unless you play a part.

Politicians cry for the "good ol' days," striking a nostalgic chord in our hearts as we remember a time in the past of remembered happiness. Many who are oppressed by the anxieties placed on them by self-satisfying but inferior bigots would ask when were the "good ol days." I don't know when they were, but, I do know better days are coming. Yes, better days are coming.

3

Part of the Solution or
Part of the Problem

Right versus Wrong versus Right

I was hired in 1988 as an appraiser for an insurance company. I caught on quite fast. The responsibilities were rather simple and routine. I would get an assignment, contact the customer and interview the person concerning his or her losses. Then I would establish an itinerary, visit locations, inspect damages and complete estimates. That was it. I did my job and did it well. For three years, with the exception of a few months, I was rated number one in productivity.

My work was good. Re-inspection of my work was completed by a re-inspector. His job was to check my work at random. Proudly, my completed assignments were all satisfactory. One morning the re-inspector stopped me as I was coming into the office.

"Oh, I've got you this time," he said overflowing with excitement.

"What is it?" I asked. He refused to tell me until the department manager was present. Finally, he arrived. The re-inspector and I hurried into his office. My estimate of damages and the re-inspection sheet were given to the manager. The re-inspector informed the manager of a mistake I had made. They both got a good laugh. I asked to see the forms.

After reviewing my estimate and the re-inspection form I concluded that it was not my calculations that were wrong. On the contrary, the re-inspector had miscalculated. The manager agreed. The re-inspector was devastated. He left the manager's office with his head hung low. I followed him to his desk.

"What is wrong, Joe?"

He told me I had to be doing something wrong, "You just can't be that good."

"Joe," I said understanding his dilemma, "Is it necessary that you find something wrong with my work?"

"Yes, boss," he replied. "You can not be that good."

Now believing that his position was established for quality control I thought that he would be happy. Strangely, I realized it was not what was written that gave him a problem. His dilemma was who wrote it. Realizing this, I offered, "Joe, if it would make you feel better, go ahead and keep the unsatisfactory, I'll be all right."

"Are you serious?" he asked. I assured him I was. I had never seen his face light up as it had that day. I rescued that rascal from the doldrums and made him happy.

That was Joe; then there was Dave.

Dave was my manager. I walked by his office, he smiled and said to keep up the good work. Usually, when I saw him, I thought of Teddy Roosevelt. Perhaps it was the thick mustache and glasses. I realized in him quiet strength. If anyone I admired made use of Roosevelt's adage, "Speak softly and carry a big stick," it was Dave. I noticed this especially on two occasions.

The first occasion was after an I-Car class. I-Car was inter-industry venture between insurance companies and repair facilities. The classes were designed to teach restorative methods and communicate new procedures and developments in the repair industry. My evenings required a demanding itinerary. I had to travel long and fast.

One night, while leaving the meeting, I was alerted by a co-worker. "Be careful," he said, "that guy said that he was going to get you." He was referring to one of the fellow students who had his share of poking fun at me.

When the guy asked who I worked for, I sarcastically gave the name of the company that he represented. The redness in his face brought no sympathy from me.

The admonition from my friend and co-worker was not taken to heart until I found myself being contemptuously penalized by my company. I was told that this guy had contacted our administration and reported my unprofessional misrepresentation of his company. Without reasonable redress, I learned that my department's director had called for my dismissal. My record of productivity and accuracy were my only refuge.

I received my evaluation, it was disappointing. Rather than focus on what I did that was right, repeated references were made to that incident. My immediate supervisor was not one to make waves. He was a conformist. In his efforts to appease the gods, the director and administration, he delivered my review for my evaluation. I received it with great concern. I went to Dave to appeal.

"Dave," I said, "it is not fair that I am still receiving punishment for my act. Nobody asked me what happened. There are at least two sides to every story. This company heard his side. No concern was given to my side."

I further explained his problem. The problem of the guy from the other company, was "not what was said as much as who said it."

Dave agreed and changed my evaluation then and there. I was later promoted to supervisor.

On another occasion, I was completing interviews with another supervisor. We were interviewing to fill my vacated slot, as well as some newly-posted appraisal positions. This supervisor's mission was self-appointed. He was to find the perfect candidate. This perfection was to be more picture perfect than perfectly qualified. His choices would serve well in magazine ads and brochures as perfect stereotypes. Young White males in white shirts were the only candidates qualified, as he confessed to giving a person a higher score because he believed the interviewee knew the answer.

On the other hand, my choices resembled the public that we served. The choices I made were not based on stereotypic ignorance that insurance adjusters were a certain kind of people. We battled over the candidates. Finally, I gave in. My uncle's admonishment, "argue with a fool against his will and find he's of the same opinion still, came true."

We took his list of names to the manager. Dave examined the list. "Donnell," he asked, "are you satisfied with these names?"

I did not want to produce any more conflicts, so I answered, "These are the names we gave you." Dave removed his glasses and asked me again with this preface, "That is not what I asked you. I want to know if you are satisfied with the names."

I stood there stunned. As well as I've used words in the past, I found myself challenged. I was speechless.

I was haunted by every misunderstanding of affirmative action and quotas. I had been demeaned by some Caucasian colleagues because I was told my job was given on the basis of affirmative action, even though Dave told me that I outscored my competitors. With a firm belief in myself, I saw within him a light of appreciation.

In my decision, I applied no affirmative action methods or reasoning. My choices were Black, White, male, female. All the candidates possessed a quality of eagerness to learn. I saw energy. It was my dream, added to their dreams, that gave me hope to create the best possible, efficient, and capable representatives in the industry.

What should I do? What should I say?

Dave broke the silence, "Take these names back and come back with some diversity. I am tired of looking at all White males."

I was elated. Of course I felt bad for those who did not get an opportunity with the company but I was excited for fairness. We left Dave's office. My desire to see the company's face, pattern the face of the community we serve, had won.

Dave also won from me a deeper respect that lives on to this day. Regretfully though, not the other supervisor. I lost someone I thought could be a friend. The other supervisor was outraged. He and I now stood equal by position. He negotiated no names. However, he did relate to me that women should not be placed in the positions we offer. I gained all but a couple of the names I first submitted. His bitterness broke our union as co-workers. I found him buried in deceit. I later witnessed his efforts to bring an end to my tenure at the insurance company.

But Have You Noticed?

Before becoming a supervisor, I was given the opportunity to enroll, at company expense, in the International Estimating Academy. I was sent with two co-workers. Each one of us represented a division that covered the state. Two hotel rooms were reserved. I, being a non-smoker, was assigned to room with the other non-smoker.

On the first night after arriving in town, we sat on the ends of our beds. Although the three of us had traveled together and had much to talk about during our trip, the two of us sat in silence. I can't remember at whose suggestion we turned on the news. It was the usual, a Black male was being arrested, handcuffed, and placed into the back of a police wagon for transport. I never understood why news reporters would so eagerly show this as news, but not show other persons of the same descent as the head of corporations, university presidents, or anything with a positive connotation.

The news never broadcast Blacks who earned scholarships or received patents. How many people in this nation, Black or White, can list five Blacks not related to sports, entertainment, politics, or religion? How many can list five Blacks who made any contribution to literature and philosophy? How many can name any Black pioneers in medicine and science? How many are familiar with inventors or explorers of color? How many minorities are Nobel Laureates? How many Americans of African descent are well-known, other than Uncle Ben and Aunt Jemima, even in cuisine?

Images, evil images, are seared on and sealed into the minds of Americans who are programmed by an imbalance of news coverage. This may explain why our judicial systems are so laden with men preoccupied with negative images and guided by bigotry. Perhaps this is why foolish American men and women of all backgrounds will, without question, continually play on the keyboard of stereotype, creating the damning refrain of doom and mistrust.

My friend, sitting on the bed next to me, having accepted these images, turned to me and asked, "You see what I mean? Why don't your people go out and get jobs like everyone else?"

Without knowing it, he had just informed me that the malignant virus of prejudice and bigotry had infected him. I quickly disinfected the room when I reminded him I was working for the same company he was. I was at the same school, for the same purpose, and because my tenure was longer, I was possibly paid more.

No one group has a bottom line description or definition. Women are women. Men are men. Whites are White. Life's beautifully creative garden was so directed and designed by the gracefully artistic hand of God so that Blacks and other American minorities span the spectrum of skin tones. Children are children. They laugh, play, and learn themselves into adulthood. Gradually they become, if allowed, senior friends of wisdom, only as old as they feel. No blanket description defines a group of people. Our diversities are only realized in our personalities, talents, tastes, political leanings, backgrounds of education, economic strengths, and philosophies of religion.

Stop Take Inventory; Think!

There are forces that lead and direct every thought and decision we make. From the moment we regain consciousness by awakening from sleep, to the very second our bodies surrender to the power of rest, we are confronted with choices. The choices we make are and will forever be influenced by our experiences. This is certainly true of the development of taste.

Whether it is by the oral sensation and identification of the things we eat and drink, choices made about the clothes we wear, the employment we seek, the places we go, or the people with whom we surround ourselves, taste is merely individual preference. Our preference is developed by what we have been acquainted with by our individual experiences. Our personal taste has a tendency to discriminate on the basis of value, complexity, and need. Let's take, for example, a typical automobile. When the majority of us make use of our buying power in the selection of transportation, we have a tendency to seek what we can afford over realizing our dream. Later, after the novelty has worn off, we often find ourselves discontent.

Here is an example:

Need versus Prejudice

Let's continue the metaphor of purchasing an automobile. It may be safely inferred that a buyer who has little money chooses the least expensive car. This person is likely to limit concerns to the following questions:

- Will this vehicle pass inspection?
- Will it leave me stranded?
- Will it meet my needs?
- Is it practical?
- Is it reliable?
- How many miles has it been driven?
- Is it fuel efficient?
- How much life is left in it?
- How will it perform?
- What will the insurance cost?

On the other hand, a person choosing to live beyond his or her means may be led by a crafty, clever, cunning, and conniving dealer who may, without calculation, care or concern, lead the buyer into the arms of a repossessor.

The less we focus on our needs, the more superficial we tend to be. A person who can afford to buy whatever he or she wants will probably consider the following questions:

- What color do I want?
- What material is available for the interior?
- What color does the interior come in?
- Is it air conditioned?
- Does it have a good sound system?
- Can I have it customized?
- Can I have it made to order?
- How will it perform?
- What kind of engine does it have?
- What are the safety features?

When a person is led by the need for transportation, it is unlikely that the color, make, or model of the vehicle will be an issue. In comparison the less we focus on or the more we are blinded to the needs of someone else, the more we tend to focus on superficials. Show me a company, an organization, a religious institution, a political party, or an institution of learning that fails to promote a healthy love and respect for all humanity, and I will predict its certain demise

Negative versus Positive

Each day we wear many hats. We exhibit many faces. Our attitudes, tolerances, and moods fluctuate according to the weather, the first person with whom we establish contact, the news, the food we eat, or even the clothes we wear. Every experience we have impacts the way we feel. The way we feel impacts the way we relate or respond to our environment.

Successfully living with one another would be realized by the establishment of a positive mental attitude. We have choices. We can fill our minds with negative or positive thoughts. The media conveys to the audience negative images that tend to distort reality. This develops the prejudice of the audience.

This was a predominating process and the success behind the election of George Bush in his 1988 bid for the White

House. Basically, Willie Horton was paraded as a Black murderer who was hand selected by Michael Dukakis to be intentionally released from prison. After his release, Horton tortured, terrorized, and murdered White females. Selling this picture to the already racially polarized public overshadowed his lack-luster effectiveness in self-promotion.

The preceding statement may offend many former Bush supporters. I personally admire President Bush; but truth is truth. The public was blinded by negative thinking. This negative thinking played on the ill-will and mistrust of people. The evil of prejudice comes between the sexes, religious faiths, political parties, generations, and economic classes. It affects everyone.

What Is Done versus Who Did It

Is it always what is done that makes the difference? Is it possible that the *who* overshadows the *what?* Think about it. Picture an ordinary checkout line, complete with a clerk and line of customers. The clerk rings up the items on the counter, the clerk gives the customer the total. The customer dishes out the money. The clerk returns the change. It is one dollar short. The variables are two people (the clerk and the customer) and the return of change.

Let's go to work.

Scenario One

The clerk is a young White female. She is neatly dressed. She is very friendly, polite, and smiles a lot. She is working to pay for a car given to her by her parents to use around campus. The customer is elderly, White, and rather affluent in her mannerisms. She exhibits well-bred charm. Her New England accent, noticed in her reference to the beautiful weather, is properly enunciated. Respect and attention is demanded of anyone sharing her personal space. "Young lady," she says summoning the clerk's attention, "you owe me one more dollar." After a few breathes of embarrassment and a couple of typical airy giggles, the clerk apologizes and hands over the dollar.

Scenario Two

The clerk is a young Black male. He is dressed in ethic garb. His hair is designed with braided dreadlocks. His voice is rather deep. His face has the look of seriousness. He is determined to do well. He is working to fulfill his dream to be the first college graduate in his family. The customer is a young White male in his thirties. He is dressed like an executive complete with trenchcoat, tie, and wing-tipped shoes. From the moment he entered the shared space of the clerk, he has been offensive.

"Say, homeboy, who do think will make the final four," he asked with the assumption that the clerk was interested in basketball. He is astonishingly coarse. After counting his change, he accuses the young man of trying to shortchange him. He calls for the manager.

What's the issue here? What happened or who did it?

Here's more:

Picture an executive who makes a miscalculation on his projections. The business that entrusted the services provided by this administrator is now seeing bottom lines in the red. It is necessary to begin corporate lay-offs. The variables are the company, the executive administrator and his miscalculations.

Scenario Three

The executive is male. He has served this company for many years. Although he inspires no creativity, he is well-educated, respected, and a rather good spirited Joe on the golf course. What should happen to him? It is now the end of the year; he receives a bonus. His call for lay-offs saved the company from ending the year in the red.

Scenario Four

The executive is female. She was newly appointed as an administrator. Her appointment was made with hopes to end the embarrassing public appearance of male domination. She has repeatedly requested statistics from the past years of operation. But her appeals were to no avail. Finally, as if by miracle, she has an idea. The idea is implemented and corporate lay-offs are not required. The company will now realize a profit before the year ends. Although many had initially wondered who she'd "slept with" to get her position, they now treat her with gratitude. She requested a bonus but was told "maybe next year."

We have been sold a bill of goods by salivating politicians who play upon the fears and abilities of the American electorate who stereotype people. The major political parties, Democrats and Republicans, sound nearly the same at center. The extremes are often exploited by self-seeking men, wheeling their evil ways through the minds making up our society, tendency to do more harm than good by misinformation.

Are there any atheist, gay, or pro-choice Republicans? Are there any fiscally-conservative and socially responsible Christian Democrats? When was the last time someone referred to the media as biased?

I've listened to radio talk shows, read newspapers and magazines, and watched television commentaries and news programs. I've heard the media being repeatedly bashed by conservatives as the "liberal media." Here is a list of people whom I have never met but who provide lessons about the "liberal medic."

> Pat Buchanan
> William F. Buckley Jr.
> Bob Grant
> Alan Keyes
> James Kilpatrick
> G. Gordon Liddy
> Rush Limbaugh
> John McLaughlin
> Oliver North
> Robert Novack
> Michael Reagan
> Pat Robertson
> William Safire
> John Sununu
> George Will
> Armstrong Williams

From whom I learned about:

> William J Bennett
> Newt Gingrich
> Jesse Helms
> Bill Kristol
> Ralph Reed

How else did I learn about the Republican contract with America? The national media as well as the local media are saturated with men and women, liberal and conservative, young and old, who have a tendency to bring themselves into the picture promoting their own prejudices.

While one religious sect prays for rain, hoping to revive its bountiful crops, another prays for sunshine. It is a constant battle of one against another. The battle is race, religious, gender, political, generational, educational, and economic warfare. To win the struggle we must learn tolerance. We must learn to appreciate our differences. We must responsibly examine our actions as we conclude how we are motivated to action. Is it what is done that we react to, or who does it?

Chauvinism: It is Not a Passing Thing

Up to this point, I have concentrated on my own personal experiences. I have recounted my early days plagued with race problems. My responses in life were often poisoned by prejudice.

Prejudice, at best, is a malignant virus with an epidemic contagion. Its pathogens spread throughout our American society and the world, maiming and killing. The germs of prejudice permeate the very soul of mankind. It is here, in man's deepest existence, that incubation occurs to later manifest itself in the mind.

The symptoms are broad. The indications are powerful. Prejudice, like AIDS, requires honest, judicious, and swift attention. The disease of prejudice is an epidemic of death that is not limited to racial matters. Race is an easy target for prejudice because it is often obvious. But what about areas of our nation and world where racial diversity is limited?

The disease of prejudice is not a passing thing. It is not genetic. It is shared long after birth, usually by parents and guardians. It may be communicated years later by contact with others so infected. It jaundices the vision and weakens one's immune system of reason. When the immune system of reason is weakened illogical inferences are made. The symptoms appear as superficially distorted and archaic opinions. These distortions and opinions come between the sexes, religious faiths, races, political persuasions, generational, educational, and economic classes. Its multiplying contagions will destroy immunity to hatred, envy, jealousy, selfishness, and cynicism. It renders the soul of humankind lifeless. It voids unconditional love and causes people to become morally obtuse. Its proportions are damning, at best. Just ask any descendant of slavery.

Chauvinism is a symptom of prejudice. It is not a passing thing. Chauvinism indiscriminately infects the mind, body, and soul of all who lack proper immunization.

Are You Immune?

The term chauvinism, in recent years, has been limited to an attitude of superiority toward members of the opposite sex, by feminists, and supporters of the women's movement. The term was best described by H.W. Cushing as, "that intolerant attitude of mind which brooks no regard for anything outside his," or her, "own circle and his," or her, "own school." Prejudice incubates chauvinism. Are you immune?

4

You've Gotta' Do It!

It Just Happened

I don't recall the day, hour, or minute I looked at myself and realized that I was FAT. I, like a number of other Americans, have a tendency to stuff the ballot box when it comes to nutrition. Sure I've peered into the looking glass and longed for my early days being, small, and skinny, but I have been fat from my earliest days.

It had to be natural selection. Nature had selected me to be awarded the flabby, full of fat, frame. At one point I tipped the scales at 310 pounds. Due to my natural construction, my bones carried it well. It was my cardiovascular system that realized hard times. Sure, I've had my share of name calling, "Fat boy," "Son of Flubber" and the best one, "Free Willy!"

Like most people, I seriously don't remember what day I crossed the line. However, I do know it took no effort to put on the weight. I also know, it takes a mindset of faith and determination in combination with a healthy diet and rigorous exercise to get rid of it. If you are overweight, I can tell you that having more than 95 pounds of useless, adiposal poundage, isn't easy. You've gotta work to get rid of it. That's right! You've got to keep the ten commandments of weight reduction.

I explain it like this:

The Ten Commandments of Weight Reduction:

1. You've gotta shove-out from that table. (Get good and healthy nutrition, but know when to quit.)

2. You've gotta change your food environment. (Get rid of those negative food influences.)

3. You've gotta watch those calories. (A few pleasures on the lips may be damning to the hips.)

4. You've gotta increase your intake of fiber and limit your intake of fat.

5. You've gotta increase your intake of water. (As noxious fluids are lost, one must maintain a heathy fluid balance.)

6. You've gotta breath good, clean, healthy, and fresh air. (Learn to appreciate the natural offerings of nature.)

7. You've gotta turn off that television, (a.k.a. "idiot box").

8. You've gotta exercise. (Move, act, exert some energy, create some heat.)

9. You've gotta shove those feet out the door. (Take an alternating half mile stroll in each possible direction of your home and get familiar with your environment. A half mile walk away and back is a one mile walk.)

10. You've gotta see yourself in reality as you are, but in faith, boldly envision the better you that you can be. (See it, believe it, achieve it)

Count the Cost

By understanding weight gain and weight loss and the difficulties attached to weight loss, we can make similar observations in our human society. Who can recall the day, hour, or minute they became bigoted, prejudiced, or chauvinistic?

Many of us find comfort and complacency in writing off our evil tendencies. We tend to negate our social responsibilities of respect by asserting we have personal opinions and preferences. However, we must realize we do trespass when our opinions and preferences begin to erode the freedoms of others.

Imagine the price we pay when we selfishly limit the freedom of personal choices made by others. What are the consequences our society must endure when others' opportunities are limited or obstructed? What is the cost of narrow-mindedly seeing our dreams as important while denying the importance or validity of others' dreams?

Seriously Think about It

How many single mothers will find it hard to raise their children because they have given up their search for adequate employment, because some bigoted person, who could have shared a decent opportunity, was guided by the stereotypic opinion, "a women's place is in the home?"

How many persons receiving public assistance would be happy, productive citizens, if they had not felt their natural rights to hopes, dreams, and attainment of success, were eradicated by the destructive and disruptive ideologies of chauvinists?

How many cases of AIDS would have never been contracted if we had not imposed disrespect and disdain on members of our communities whose sexual identities do not conform to the norms of a so-called Judeo-Christian ethic?

How many teen pregnancies would not have occurred if we valued women in our society and did not commonly accept points of view that limit the self-respect and self-esteem of females?

How many prisons would have their populations reduced if societal fairness was the rule and not the exception, if American justice was not steeped in prejudice?

How many wars would have been averted if someone had simply granted respect to the right of an opposing point of view?

How many senior citizens could live in peace, knowing that some young, newly elected, wet-behind-the-ears, member of Congress was not out to blame them for the economic woes of our nation and fighting to reduce their security?

So many times, we well-meaning, self-centered, self-interested, moralists have unknowingly set minefields, limiting our own freedoms by the explosive fears of backlash. Count the costs. Failure to work with and realize the condition of the social body is just as dangerous, if not more dangerous than neglect of the personal body. It is more dangerous because neglect of one's personal body can only harm one person. Neglect of the social body can destroy masses of people.

Most of us, particularly American citizens, have been tricked from every conceivable angle as to why life presents the difficulties it does. The source of our difficulties can often be found by looking in one's own mirror. We have learned to tolerate the dregs by people who avail themselves to the evils of prejudice. We have been lulled into a daze by vipers whose venomous opinions mold, shape, and direct the paths in which we walk.

Without question, void of thought, we have fattened ourselves with negative information of all descriptions. We have been supplied with a feast of misleading information by the media. We have wined and dined ourselves into a gluttonous and drunken stupor by the feast and spirits of prejudice. Our personal opinions have become isolated from the truth of the goodness of civilization.

Time for Pardon

There is a time and a season for everything under heaven. In America, although often neglected, there is a time to vote. In America, we are afforded the privilege of the ballot box. We can choose our leaders. We elect leaders of our local community associations to the president of our nation. By trivializing this important gift of civilization, a cancer has developed and is compromising the health of our democracy.

Many of our elected officials have flagrantly prostituted themselves to corporations and political action committees, lining their pockets with money for evil. Even though many of us are fully aware of this, we press on to elect whoever, by which dollar, puts on the best promotion. Some are turned off by the dog show of American politics and have ceased to participate. Some apathetically feel, why bother? They find in our leaders nothing to with they can relate. In some cases, this is good. In all cases, it destroys the privileges of a democracy.

The privilege to vote in America is also tainted by evils of bigotry, chauvinism, and prejudice. This opportunity and benefit, afforded by our democracy, has been trivialized by petty evil. People of color wait with baited breath for the day that the White House will no longer be called, or noticed as, the "White" House or, more direct, the "White Man's House." Many women, liberal and conservative, long for the day when the person elected to hold this office will not be addressed as "Mr. President," but as "Ms. President." Others would elect anyone to clear the national consciousness of the misdeeds of its heritage.

How many White Americans were ready and willing to elect General Collin Powell to serve as President of this great nation? For many, this choice was made once they realized that he would not run. Without a clue to his positions or views, General Powell paraded up, down and across the minds of the American electorate so forcefully that many failed to question his opinions, or worst, his vision of America's future. Seemingly, if America can elect a man of color, a woman, or anyone else currently locked out of a position of power, prestige and prominence, America would be absolved of all her past crimes against humanity.

No one who has not committed or allowed atrocities that have been levied against humanity needs to be pardoned. However, if one can not look into the mirror with full knowledge and confidence that he or she has never committed sins of disrespect, no matter how small or seemingly insignificant, then he or she is party to the problems that cause much of the disunity in our world and need to be absolved. Don't wait for some public person to lift the torch and do it. You do it!

You Have Gotta Do It

If America is to be a better nation, it will be on my back as well as yours. We are responsible for formulations and designs for the achievement of a lasting social peace. This book is a plea, first to the soul of America and then to the world.

It is first to America because the author is American. That's right! No matter what anyone else says, I am an American. I was born to parents who are Americans and themselves the progeny of Americans. It is my firmest belief that before I or anyone should attempt to preach peace in the world, one should begin this sermon at home. I must first challenge my nation. I must confront my home. I've gotta' do it!

5

My America, My World, My Hope

On America

From the shorelines of the Atlantic to the Pacific, America is a land full of natural beauties. It's snowcapped mountains and luscious green valleys provide wonders upon wonders of the artistically sculptured and creative design of God. Among its natural beauties is its lavish garden of humanity.

America, like no other nation, has been blessed to the extreme with diversity. Its rainbow of earthen skintones spans the spectrum of hues from albino to rich, dark coffee. Its language is a formulation bearing the expressions of every region on earth. Its taste for food ranges from simple southern rice and beans, to aromatic western mesquite smoked barbecued spareribs.

If one were to inquire, what is the American taste, there is no single answer. If one were to inquire of its appetite, it would be international: African, Australian, Caribbean, Greek, Italian, Oriental, Mexican, Salvadoran, Polish, Russian, Kosher, and so on. The taste of this nation is an international palate.

The arts of America are regionally expressed in architecture, sculpture, painting, and handicrafts of all kinds. The music ranges from the symphonic sound of Boston, the blues of New Orleans, the choral sound of Salt Lake City, to the Opera of New York. Its music is the happy jazz of New

Orleans, the cool jazz of Memphis, and the trumpeted jazz of St. Louis. It's the rock of Chicago and the rap of L.A. It is the soul of Detroit, to the sound machine of Miami. The American sound is the Bluegrass of Kentucky, the gospel of Atlanta, the blues of Mississippi. It is the harmony of Nashville. From the spirituals which buoyed the hope of the slaves, to the Anthems of praise echoed in the cathedrals, this nation offers exquisite richness of sound.

America, my America, is the vision of the experienced and the hopeful dreams of the young. It is the land of expansion by development, creativity, and invention. America is an answer to the demand for life, liberty, and the pursuit of happiness.

I love my nation, but somehow, with all its beauties, gifts of diversity, and promise, America must hang its head in moral shame. While preaching political sermons, it avoids the lesson of love. For money, she has auctioned her soul. On her quest for power, she has been prostituted to evil and deceit by the pimps of injustice. This mother of exiles has a flaw in character. It is hidden behind welcoming arms hypocritically calling, "Give me your tired, your poor, your huddled masses yearning to breathe free, the wretched refuse of your teeming shore. Send these, the homeless, tempest-tossed to me, I lift my lamp beside the gold door!"

Today, moves are afoot by conservative political leaders to be bigoted, prejudiced, isolationist. By their theories of nationalism, they rush to slam shut the open and welcoming doors of this nation. Is it possible that they have forgotten this nation was begun by imposing colonizers who forced open unwelcoming doors, creating a nation of immigrants?

This is a nation that, while having a population of poor, calls for the poor. Somewhere deep in the storehouses of historical memory is a container of compassion. This compassion was delivered as a gift of the Judeo-Christian heritage. Somehow, by the jaded rush of selfishness and superficiality, most in our nation have forgotten compassion.

This is a nation that, while having huddled masses in its inner-cities yearning to breathe free, calls for more. This nation lives with dangers from within as guns and drugs fill its streets. Here is found corruption by leaders pimping its pride and promise, prostituting the citizenry to whomever bids the highest dollar.

By the torch held high by that lady in New York harbor, this nation, having wretched and homeless, calls for more. America offers safety for the tempest-tossed. This was the motivating force in the mind of Emma Lazarus who authored the sonnet, "The New Colossus." From this sonnet is the inscription on the base of the Statue of Liberty. It is the song of her faith in America as a haven for the oppressed.

But Wasn't Slavery Oppressive?

Yes it was! Just twenty-three years before the statue's inscription the Emancipation Proclamation was signed. Many believe this was a legal end to the damnable institution of slavery. It was not. It specifically declared slaves within any state in rebellion to the Union, free. But it exempted slaves in parts of the South then held by the Union Armies.

Long before the rise of slavery, America had bedded herself with greed. It was the Native Americans who first realized the brutality and savagery of the new settlers. These settlers were the new immigrants to their world. They came, they saw, they conquered without respect to the residents of north America. Without invitation, they came. Their eyes were bulging, greedy for America's bounty. Without welcome, they polluted the streams, poisoned the fish, raped the maidens, brutally murdered the chiefs, burned villages, and maimed sons with the grandiose announcement that civilization had arrived.

Long fatalistic voyages over rough and stormy seas had taken their toll. Many of the newly-established residents of this frontier were so worn out by the long excursions and battles of thievery, that they lacked energy and drive to till the soil. It was either for this reason, or extreme laziness, that required and gave economy to the market of slaves.

The history of America is a history of greatness, strength and will. Stored away or hidden deep, buried below the soil of the American conscience is compassion. However, it is distorted by the dark clouds of injustice which roots itself in chauvinistic alliances with bias, bigotry, and prejudice. How can our lady survive in the harbor? How can we be a shining city on a hill? How can we lead the world in truth, justice, and peace if we can not safeguard these natural rights at home? As I see it, America is a diverse microcosm of the world.

My World As I See It

By appearance, the world is a radiant blue marble inlaid with oceans, seas, and lands engulfed by a continuously changing circle of clouds. Despite its enormous size, the inventions of travel and technology, have reduced the globe to fit figuratively into the cradling palm of a baby.

The world is populated by humans who differ in body as well as thought. Many find it good to hold each other at odds and exploit these differences. Noticing this, the world may be described as a common thread of community wound tightly into a global ball of intense struggle.

Here I sit at my desk, looking out my window. I notice the passing of cars, constant in one direction or another. By the roadside is a line of trees and homes whose heights create a skyline. Just above is a boundless horizon. It has no beginning or end. It is all away, far, distant from the earth's core. Compared with its distance is the collective power harnessed by the soul, the will, and the mind of man.

The Soul and Spirit of Man

We, inhabitants of the world, are a collection of spiritual beings bound in mortal bodies. This is my explanation of soul. Our souls are a kinship by the universal language of emotion. This explains why our emotions are not restrained by the barriers of language and dialect. We all have a sense of humor. When the strings of our emotion are plucked in familiar ways of amusement, we laugh. Conversely, when our bodies or spirits are racked with pain, as in the loss of a loved one, our emotions promote tears. Without learning, babies throughout our world laugh and cry. As they develop, they learn by societal mores what is worthy of a laugh and what permits a tear.

There are some who develop cheerfully. They are magnetic and charismatic in their unions with others. On the contrary, men and women develop from the harsh foundations of indifference and neglect. Many of them developed as cold and calloused, bearing the scars of painful experiences.

We are spiritual beings bound in mortal bodies. While we can splint the broken body or bandage torn flesh, we have great difficulties healing the wounded soul. For this reason, we must be careful of the injuries we inflict.

The Will of Man

Our world is full of spiritual beings, nearly five billion in all. We are spiritual beings with a will. By forces distant from the thoughts of man, our wills are a balance in the protection and survival of humanity.

Our will is an intangible determination of desire, choice, consent, or refusal, known as one's willingness of internal or external thought. Each second of life, the working mind of a human is controlled by the impulses of thought. Our thoughts are in a constant struggle with good and evil. Our thoughts are always weighing and balancing choices.

Our choices are determined by learned values balanced against levels of selfishness. Our values are reflective of our personal alignments and community-learned mores. Our levels of selfishness are contingent upon our learned degrees of respect.

From the first flicker of flame, to the international answer of a call on the Internet, the human mind has been a wonderful journey of evolution. Humans wandered from caves which gave shelter and safety from the elements. They wandered over vast frontiers, endless, fruitful, and fertile bodies of land, taking residence wherever they chose. From the dwellings of tents, mankind immigrated into communities where dwellings of permanence were established. No matter which racial or ethnic community with which you are identified, regardless of age, sex, political, or religious persuasion, we are all related. We are family. By the union of God and the oneness of family, we have hope.

Creation versus Evolution and the Mind

Although I firmly believe in the intelligent and planned creation of humans, I do believe in evolution. Further, I believe any intelligent theist, or believer in God and the Genesis record of creation, would understand the principles supporting my belief.

First to my theistic friends, creationists and believers in God, Charles Darwin was right with his theory of Natural Selection. It was God who, having selected the finest in natural clay, molded into His image and likeness the body of man. Into the nostrils of this sculpture designed of God's natural selection was blown the very breath of its creator. If the story of Adam and Eve is literally true what accounts for the variations of humans are found throughout the world? Why the differences of race and body structure?

As humans moved across the regions of earth, the natural environment differed. Mankind was scattered over the deserts, lifted by mountains, burned by the equator, and chilled by the poles. For the survival of humans, man was forced to adapt. The constant change of natural community resulted in the evolution of man. I call this Adaptive Evolution.

Although our bodies are naturally stamped by region, bearing marks of difference, we are still family. The missing link of commonality is God, and in Him is our hope.

6

Our Trust, Our Faith,
Our Only Hope

Religion is a person's foundation of practice, scaffolding his or her system of beliefs, principles and faith. It is the causal by-product of one's basic presuppositions learned by environmental upbringing from a series of experiences.

Our religious ideologies are molded by our experiences borne by our environments. For many, it has become a supernatural alignment with an infinite form of intelligence. It is the structure for attitudes, likes, and dislikes. It is the foundation of societal mores and an invitation to conformity. Religion, when used positively, brings hope to despair, laughter to tears, and knowledge to ignorance, thus lighting the path which leads from darkness. Religion is ultimately a person's way of life in their relationship with the universe. Religion is a guide which moves a person from life to death with consciousness of an after life.

Religion makes no one good or evil. Good and evil are based on our rights of free choice. We are confronted by constant choices. Some choices are good. They are good in reasoning and outcome. The outcomes can support the individual or society. Some choices are detrimental to the individual, the society, or both. A detrimental use of religion is not necessarily evil, as much as it is destructive. When destructive, it serves no purpose other than to mirror our ways and allow us the choice for change. Likewise, we are free to choose our own religion.

In the western world, especially America, the majority of those who practice under the name of an organized religion practice Judaic, Islamic, or Christian teachings. These three religious beliefs are common in their views as theistic. Theism is a belief in a God. Simply put, these three religions are communities of faith. Although there are many types, persuasions, and leanings in each, their faiths are usually a conformity to a pattern of thought. This thought process is a foundation for societal codes.

While the United States of America boasts of separation of Church and State, it is certain that its moral, civil, political, and judicial laws, written and unwritten, are heavily influenced by religion. This is good! However, teachers and practitioners are not perfect. Many practitioners and leaders of faith have amalgamated into their teachings bigotries, prejudices, and twists of chauvinism. Many followers have dangerously accepted these flawed teachings. These followers have themselves become teachers. This diminishes the hope that religion offers.

Biblically, James, a New Testament author and a brother of Christ, challenging followers of Christ's teachings to express their faith in their daily lives wrote, "If anyone considers himself religious and does not keep a tight rein on his tongue, he deceives himself, and his religion is worthless." Religion that God accepts as right and pure is this: to look after the orphans and widows in their distress and to keep one's self from being polluted by the world.

Real religion shows concern for the downtrodden and respect for the right of choice. True religion is self-control. Religion is a personal decision, regardless of the world around. True religion is the kept-promise between a person and that person's God.

Sadly, Charles Colton was right when he wrote, "Men will wrangle for religion, write for it, fight for it, die for it; anything but live for it." Similarly Jonathan Swift wrote in his, "Thoughts on Various Subjects," that "We have just enough religion to make us hate, but not enough to make us love one another."

I applaud the atheist who announces to the world his or her inability to comprehend or believe in the physical or spiritual existence of God. This is so much more honest than the theist who totes baggage packed with hate.

Enough of intolerance and disrespect; we need good, clean, healthy religion. If this world is to survive, we had better get it fast. True religion is our only hope!

Healing for the Nation

As I listen to the news and make my way through the print media. I have concluded our world is sick. Wounded by selfishness, it lays at the brink of death. The social heart that once pumped love is now poisoned by a virus of hate. Life monitors seem only to record economic and political readings. Neglected are children and the unborn, the promise of its future. Leaders let selfish greed stand in the way of America's survival.

While Catholics and Protestants seek to annihilate each other in Ireland, while Muslims and Jews duke it out in the Mideast, while Koreans, Chinese, and Taiwanese battle in the Orient, the life of our world is being lost. In America, the poison is materialism and power. In South Africa, the cure is a right to vote. Drug wars in South America and territorial wars in Europe are destroying the life of our world.

While adults fight, children die of hunger. Children are orphaned by war. Wives become widows. As fighting continues a legacy is being created. The legacy is a world history affirming our inability to get along.

America is a nation of experiment. With its diversities of every type, it is an image of the world. If America can make it; the world can make it. America is engulfed in strife and struggle. America is a chasm, an open, oozing, cancerous sore of contention. America has a history of racial unrest. No one leader of this nation has ever had the nobility to publicly

apologize for the use of slaves and denial of basic civil rights
to its citizenry of African descent. America is shameful for its
treatment of women. For centuries, it has denied women the
right to choose and succeed, equal with men. If a woman does
make it to the top, you can be certain there will be a man
there to whom she must answer.

America is a nation whose blood flows rich with the
poisons of bigotry. Intolerance is its by-product creating le-
gions of hate and neglect. As our streets overflow with violence, drugs, illiteracy, teen pregnancy, suicide, political unrest, and all other negativities, one may find a spark of hope.
It is seen in the eyes of tomorrow. The eyes of tomorrow are
the children. Our children will lift America from its critical
condition. A child will nurse health into our society. It is the
vitality of my home, my America, that will lift the world from
the brink of death. There is healing for the nation. This
healing is the hope of our world.

A Commonality of Hope

Earlier in this chapter is a reference to the theist. These
are believers in God. Regardless of specific religious identification, theists find a common hold on much of the Old Testament of the Bible.

In the Old Testament, 2 Chronicles 7:14 reads, "If God's
people who are called by His name, will humble themselves
and pray, and seek God's face and turn from their wicked
ways; then God will hear from heaven and will forgive their
sin and will heal their land." All men search for lasting peace.
In this search, the answer comes from God and His people.

Who Are God's People?

I am reminded of a story I once heard. It was about a
little boy who, having saved his money, walked into a pet
store and purchased a bird. This little fellow had been eyeing
this bird for some time. Finally, the bird was his, or so he
thought. Once the bird was delivered to him, he was on his
way. With joy and excitement he shouted, "It's mine, it's
mine!" The little boy was very responsible. Each day he fed

and cared for his bird. It was certain that he loved his little friend. One day as he opened the cage, the little bird escaped and flew away. The little boy was sad. Actually, he was devastated. His Dad offered to buy him another bird. But another bird would never replace the bird he had lost.

Day after day when he returned from school, he would call for his bird. Evening after evening he went to his yard and called. He tweeted, he whistled, trying to imitate the bird's sound. He called his bird's name. His bird was not in sight.

One evening, as the little boy sat just outside the door, he heard a sound. "Tweet! Tweet! Tweet!" He looked up and perched on a post nearby was his feathered friend.

No matter what price, no matter what sacrifice was made for ownership of this bird, it was not the possession of the little boy. No matter how caged or captured, the boy could claim no ownership of the bird. The bird belonged to itself. The wide, open, boundless sky was its home. Not until the bird found its way back, could this little boy have the bird. I am not writing to persuade anyone to believe as I do. My purpose is peace. I want my home and world involved in an ongoing project of peace.

Who are God's people? God's people are his creations which have found their way back to God. If you claim to be called by His name, then you just may be. I believe there are enough people in this world making this claim. They are enough to make a difference.

Our religion is our trust and our faith. A positive, clean, respectful, and tolerant religion is our only hope.

7

Steps to Peace

Just what is peace? In recent years, peace has taken on many personalities. Politically speaking, peace has become the right to free speech. No matter how disrespectful or alienating, free speech has been emphasized. From this wasteland of thought is the development of superiority. It is here that peace is believed to be the right of suppressing or annihilating those who are dissimilar to one's self or one's community. But this peace is selfish. Selfishness is unkind, self-seeking, self-promoting, self-gratifying, and oppressive. Peace on this level becomes a mask of deception. It covers the face of fear. This fear torments the mind and becomes the backbone of bigotry and prejudice. It is here that this negative form of deceptive peace enslaves anyone who follows its teachings.

Real peace results in a state of security for all of humanity. It dignifies life through the bountiful expressions of freedom. Real peace is harmony in relationships to the establishment of mutual respect, not to be confused with mutual agreement. Real peace is freedom from personal and social oppression. Real peace will free our world from civil unrest and disturbance.

How Do We Find Peace?

While nothing is wrong with the possession of wealth, we must be mindful of its negative by-products. The cunning call of material success and prosperity has for many resulted in the creation of selfishness. Many who witness a spark of materialism are ignited into selfish flames of passionate greed. Greed violates freedom. No one on this level can achieve peace. Not even the self-gratifying materialist who must spend his days devising methods and ways for security can find peace.

There is a road that leads to peace but there are only a few who find it. With the amassing of wealth, peace is unattainable. The road to peace is long. It is sought by many. No vehicle will transport the traveler who follows this road. The only way to reach its end is to walk.

Physically, the road to peace has a surface which is neglected. It has potholes and is laden with cracks. It is a winding path of uncertainty. Its sides are lined by a deep, dark, and foreboding forest. Hidden within its brush are hijackers, muggers, and robbers seeking a prey of peacekeepers. The mission of these bad men is to turn back as many travelers as possible. Success in turning back peace seekers destroys the noble desire for peace. Strategically, this road has been mined and is under constant attack.

When night falls, a strange spirit comes to life. The road to peace seemingly becomes haunted. Spirits of challenge howl in voices reminiscent of history. The noble voices of fairness, respect, and opportunity remind us of bloody battles which resulted in the loss of life. We avoid peace, and in its place, we become warriors. The wind blows and riding upon its currents are echoes of people who lived and died. They were martyrs who lived and died attempting to guide us on the path of peace.

Achieving peace is not impossible, impractical, or unachievable. Peace is self-determination and decision met by challenge. If the goal is clear, focused, and the rights of others are sustained, preserved, and protected, seekers of peace become the authors of a guarantee which makes reaching peace a certainty.

So What Is Peace?

Simply put, peace is a tranquil state of relaxation. The ability to achieve peace is comparable to the talents of painters, sculptors, musicians, and inventors. Peace is a cultivated ability to hear, high above the noises and distractions of life, the soft, sweet melody of a sparrow. Peace is freedom from fear. Finally, peace is kindness, certitude, and justice.

Enemies of Peace

Peace has many enemies that obstruct it. One of the greatest enemies to peace is fear. Fear is the lack of security. In the presence of fear, humans are prone to war. This is a naturally-learned technique of survival. Fear is the backbone of superiority that develops and promotes prejudice and bigotry. A logical byproduct of fear is chauvinism. Many throughout our world have learned to live in fear. Many men fear women. Likewise, many women fear men. Many question the intent and fairness of the opposite sex. This may be one of the causes of homosexuality. It may further be one of the causes of the figurative glass ceiling which denies women top status in our society.

Then there are generation gaps, a by-product of fear. Many of our young distrust aged members of society. Their mistrust is supported by fear. Many of those considered chronologically young in our society believe the older members are prone to betrayal and are envious of youth. Likewise, many of the senior members create disunity by creating and adhering to negative stereotypes. These stereotypes strip the canvas of the intelligence, abilities, hopes, and dreams of our young. In its place are images of moral decline and shame.

By the same principles, many Whites fear Blacks and many Blacks fear Whites. Both groups, although they work together, go to school together and shop together tend to favor isolationism. If you doubt this, visit most American churches, which should be teaching brotherhood and sisterhood, on Sunday morning. Americans, for the most part, have a fear of aliens and immigrants. This fear is a major cause behind those seeking to become isolationists. Fear is also displayed within the religious realm as Protestants and Catholics fear and hate each other, for example, in Ireland.

Why can't believers of God find common ground? Why do most theistic practitioners spend so much time negatively finding points to discredit each other? It is because of fear. Fear is the obstacle that disallows them the freedom to point out what is right with the other.

Another fear that stands in the way of peace is the fear of displacement. This fear causes many stresses. This fear may be the greatest cause behind discrimination. Many in middle- and upper-management have learned not to appreciate the employment and empowerment of gifted persons whose abilities may outweigh their own. Failure to suppress this fear challenges the quality of the American products and lowers our ability to compete strongly in a world market. The fear of displacement also calls for protectionism. Laws and high tariffs are required to limit the importation of goods. You would logically think this fear would better the quality and durability of American products. It does nothing of the sort.

Pride Versus Prejudice

Finally, fear is the moth that slowly eats away the fabric of the brotherhood. Being an American is a real blessing. But along with the blessings of being an American, especially an American of African descent, I have learned that our fears cause us to distrust others, especially those who are dissimilar to ourselves. Americans play up and prey on every fear and stereotype known to mankind. Our fears cause us to negatively describe and complain about the slant-eyed, round headed, yellow skinned Japanese. We claim that they are buying up too much American real estate. Is it damage levied against American pride and property that supports the cries or are the cries echoes of prejudice? While many Americans claim to deplore the sale of the nation, unfairly the Japanese are singled out. European investment into American properties far outweighs Japanese investment. Yet the Europeans have not created a crisis.

Fear has caused many African-Americans to hate the so-called, "White man." Many believe it is the White man's mission to destroy the very soul of the Black man. While this may be true of some Whites, it is not representative of all Caucasians. This belief overshadows the fact that one of the America's oldest civil rights organizations was begun by the union of Blacks and Whites.

The extreme mistreatment of Blacks in America resulted in a riot in 1908, in Springfield, Illinois, the hometown of Abraham Lincoln, where the White citizens had attempted to eliminate Black residents. The National Association for the Advancement of Colored People (NAACP) was formed. In 1909, at New York City, Blacks, in union with Whites, formed the NAACP for the purpose of alleviating the evil, untenable conditions under which Americans of African descent lived. Sixty people, Black and White, convened on Lincoln's birthday, February 12th, to form the NAACP. Is it Black pride or Black fear, on the back of willful mistreatment, that prejudices most African American minds against working with or tolerating White Americans?

Likewise, fear has caused many White Americans to live in constant fear of dark-skinned Americans. What else would account for its preoccupation with its southern border, but not its northern border? What else would cause a White person to lock the car door at a traffic stop when a Black man is standing on a corner, but not when a White man is seen? What would account for the decision, when running late, to wait for another elevator rather than ride with a Black male? Further, most of the animosities and hostilities causing discord and conflict are not because of acts against one another, but fears of each other. These fears are due to the suppression of truth and a widespread acceptance of stereotypes. Many people in White America are ignorant of the fact that many of the luxuries and securities they have are developments of American people of African descent and extraction.

Social Contributions by African Americans

Why are the majority of persons held behind prison walls in America Black, when statistics show the majority of crimes are committed by Whites? How is it believed that Blacks are more dangerous than Whites when the overwhelming major-

ity of serial killers are White? Most crimes committed by
Blacks are against Blacks. Could the American media be responsible by presenting Black America in a negative light?
Could corporate advertisers be responsible, by promoting the
ideal American as White? Could the government be responsible by fighting the war on drugs mainly in the inner-cities
and heavily populated Black areas? Could our public schools
be responsible by neglecting to educate students about Blacks'
contribution to American society and depicting the sole con-
tributors as White?

I recently asked friends to name five nations of Europe.
I got answers like:

> Germany
> Great Britain
> France
> Italy
> Spain

Then I would ask for five nations of Asia. In response I
would hear:

> Japan
> China
> Korea
> Vietnam
> Philippines

Then I would ask for the 5 nations on the continent of
South America. They would respond with:

> Argentina
> Brazil
> Chile
> Colombia
> Venezuela

(Many times, Mexico would be included in the five South
American nations. Many had no clue that Mexico was part of
the continent of North America.) But, when I asked them to
name five countries in Africa, many thought Africa was a

country. When they were reminded of it being a continent with many countries, most could name only South Africa as a country.

Africa is a continent of nations such as Morocco, Algeria, Libya, and Egypt. Those nations are home to people like Hosne Muburak, Moamar Kadafi, Desmond Tutu, Alan Bozak, and Nelson Mandela. Many times, Africa is seen as a vast land of huts or the setting for safaris. It is a rich part of our world. In America, many sons and daughters of former slaves helped to establish and make our nation great.

In 1770, Crispus Attucks, a descendent of slaves, at the young age of 47, was the first American to die in the struggle for American independence. This battle was later known as the Boston Massacre. It opened the door to the Revolutionary War which won the United States of America its freedom to govern itself as it desired.

In 1731, near Baltimore, Maryland, Benjamin Banneker, a Black man, was born. At the age of 22, he produced the first wooden clock ever built in the United States. It was made entirely of wood, every gear was carved by hand. His clock kept perfect time. It struck every hour for more than forty years. The news of this clock stirred such a sensation that people came from all over to see it and the Black genius who made it.

Banneker's major reputation stems from his service as a surveyor on the six man team which helped design the blueprints for Washington, DC. President Washington had appointed Banneker to the DC planning and construction commission making him the first Black presidential appointee in the United States. He helped in the selection of sites for the U.S. Capitol building, the U.S. Treasury building, the White House, and other Federal buildings. When the chairman of the civil engineering team, Major L'enfant, abruptly resigned and returned to France with the plans, Banneker's photographic memory enabled him to reproduce them in their entirety. Washington DC, with its grand avenues and buildings, was completed and stands today as a monument to Banneker's genius.

In 1848 Lewis Latimer was born. He was a pioneer in the development of the electric light bulb. He was the only Black member of the Edison Pioneers, a group of distinguished scientists and inventors who worked with Thomas Edison. Prior to his work with Edison, he had been noticed as a highly skilled draftsman. The patent solicitor firm of Crosby and Gould employed him as their chief draftsman. Around 1876, Alexander Graham Bell recognized his need for a highly-skilled draftsman to prepare blueprints for his new invention, the telephone. Bell went to Crosby and Gould. It was Lattimer who was given the assignment to draw plans for Bell's telephone patent.

In 1875, Garrett Morgan was born. He is best known for his invention of the automatic traffic signal. His invention brought order to chaos in the nation's streets and improved traffic safety. He also invented a gas mask widely used by fireman in the early 1900s and by soldiers on the battlefields of Europe during World War I.

On the night of July 25, 1916, a tunnel being constructed under Lake Erie exploded, leaving many workers of the Cleveland Water Works trapped. Some workers lost their lives in this tragedy. Morgan and his brother Frank were called. Wearing gas masks, they, with two other volunteers, courageously entered the tunnel. The fire and police officials were afraid to do so. They all emerged safely and many lives were saved.

In 1892, Frederick James was born. James was the inventor of the first practical refrigeration system for long haul trucks. His system was later adapted to a variety of other means of transportation including ships and railway cars. This Black native of Cincinnati, Ohio was orphaned at the age of nine years and never managed to get more than a sixth grade education. During World War I, in France, he served as an electrician in the U.S. Army. He achieved the rank of sergeant. The crisis of World War II inspired James to design a special refrigeration unit that would keep blood serum fresh for emergencies such as transfusions and for medicines. In 1961, at Minneapolis, MN, he died, credited with more than

60 patents, forty for refrigeration equipment alone. His invention completely changed the food transport industry. It allowed for international shipment of food.

In 1894 Lloyd Hall was born. He was a pioneer in the industrial food chemistry. He revolutionized the meat packing industry with his development of curing salts for the processing and preservation of meats. His patented chemical processes also benefited other food products. He was successful in new sterilization techniques for food and spices. He used ethylene oxide gas in a vacuum chamber with foods, effectively sterilizing them and enhancing their appearance, quality, and flavor. Hall's method of sterilization with ethylene oxide became a big business in the United States for hospital supplies, such as bandages, dressings, denitrifices, cosmetics, and other products.

In 1899, Percy Julian was born. This son of a railway mail clerk and a teacher, was an organic chemist . He taught at Fisk University before entering Harvard University, where he received a Master's Degree in chemistry. He later traveled to Vienna there he studied for his Ph.D. While there, he became interested in research of soybeans. At his alma mater, DePaul University in Greencastle, Indiana, Dr. Julian, along with his assistant, Dr. Pikl, were the first to synthesize physostigmine, a drug used in the treatment of glaucoma. Dr. Julian also saved thousands of lives with his invention of the "aero-foam," which was derived from soybeans. It was used to extinguish fires. Dr. Julian also discovered a more economical way to extract sterols from soybean oil to produce sex hormones. Dr. Julian is probably best known for the development of a way of synthetically producing cortisone in large quantities at a reasonable cost. Before his discovery, cortisone, used in the treatment of rheumatoid arthritis, was available only in limited quantities and was extremely expensive.

In 1904, Dr. Charles Richard Drew was born. He was a renowned surgeon, medical scientist, educator, and authority on the preservation of blood. He was the pioneer of blood plasma preservation. He left mankind an important legacy: the blood bank. During World War II, England suffered heavy casualties and called upon Dr. Drew to initiate its military blood bank program. There he introduced preserved blood on the battlefield. This system worked so well that the British asked him to organize the world's first mass blood bank project. He also became the first Director of the American Red Cross. He taught us that, although our blood may differ in types, there was no scientific basis to indicate any difference in human blood on the basis of race. Dr. Drew was killed in an automobile accident while on a trip to a medical meeting at the Tuskegee Institute in 1950. The irony of his death is that his life may have been saved, if he had received immediate medical attention following his accident. Discrimination at nearby White hospitals did not allow him the blood transfusions needed to save his life.

In 1910, Granville T. Woods died, but not before being awarded more than 150 patents, thirty five for his electrical innovations alone, which left him a legacy of being known as the, "Black Edison." This native of Columbus, Ohio, attended school to age ten. Yet his genius for modifying and improving electrical apparatuses was unsurpassed during the Industrial Revolution.

In 1881, Woods opened a factory in Cincinnati, Ohio where he manufactured telephones, telegraphs, and electrical equipment. Three years later, he filed his first application for a patent. This patent was for an improved steam boiler furnace. Later in 1884, he invented a telephone transmitter. His transmitter could carry the voice over a longer distance with greater clarity and more distinct sound. A year later, Woods patented an apparatus he coined "telephony," a combination of the telephone and telegraph. As a result, telegraph stations could send both oral and signal messages over the same line. This enabled an inexperienced telegraph operator to send messages without the benefit of knowing Morse Code.

In 1887, Woods produced one of his most important inventions. It was a device known as the Synchronous Multiplex Railway Telegraph. It enabled messages to be sent to and from moving trains and railway stations. Serious accidents were avoided because conductors could now be warned of obstacles in their paths.

Woods was also responsible for modernizing our transportation system. He invented an overhead conducting system for electric railways still utilized by trains and trolley cars today. He also invented the electrified "third rail," now used by subway systems in large cities throughout America.

Many contributions advancing our world are legacies of Black genius. They have gifted our society and expanded our civilization. If you are not a descendant of Africa, remember this. The next time you enter a space shared by an African American and become overwhelmed with fear, remember that although most Americans of African descent are depicted in negative and stereotypic ways, it was their minds, no different than yours, that made life a little easier, a little healthier, a little brighter, a little closer, a little more secure, a little stronger, a little tastier, and better for us all.

A Simple Lesson from Granddad

In response to my frustration with White America and their offenses, then Black America and its offenses, then White and Black America, and how they both seem to frustrate, my granddaddy said, "Donny, good and bad people come in all makes and colors. You be careful to do what is right."

You can not control others. Statements defining the actions of a specific group only play on the stage of stereotype. Even if blanket statements, which are mainly negative, were accurate, there is not much you could do to change it. No matter what is done you, just be certain to do what is right. This is wisdom from my granddad.

8

An Ordinance for Peace

A Moral and Civil Code of Conduct

A few months after the Exodus, when the Israelis escaped the bondage of Egypt, these chosen people of God were led to set up a desert camp at the bottom of a mountain called Sinai. It was from this camp that their leader and minister to the people, Moses, left on a hiking expedition to the mountain top's. The people camped below were inhibited by fear to follow. It is recorded that the presence of God was made known in a very dramatic and frightening way. People were not allowed to approach the mountains. Trespassers were to be stoned or shot to death. Not until the resonate blast of a trumpet would humans or animals be permitted to proceed beyond the limits allowing passage up the mountain.

Three days after Moses went up the mountain, the campers witnessed a descent of thick cloud complete with brilliant bolts of lightning and quaking, roaring, rolls of thunder. This cloud had the appearance of smoke which seemed to billow upward spitting out sparks and flames, as if from a furnace. It was believed to be a sign of God. The leader and representative of this displaced family of wandering campers found himself engulfed in fear. Moses was allowed, but only to a certain point, the support and companionship of his Jewish brother and spokesman, Aaron.

On this mountain, God conferred with humanity. God physically made his presence known while in conversation with humans. It was here that God spoke and confirmed, in writing, the moral and civil codes to govern this new nation of people. These laws are known today as the Ten Commandments.

These commandments are specific. They are guidelines of respect first to God, then to humanity. To paraphrase from the Bible, Exodus, chapter 20 and Deuteronomy, chapter four, where these laws are biblically listed, God declared:

You would not be where you are today had I not delivered you from your captors who enslaved you.

1. You must respect God as the ultimate existence of life;

2. Do not idolize anything. If you do, you become the author and granter of your own curse;

3. You must respect God's name and reputation or be punished for the guilt of perverting its use;

4. You may work six days, but you must set aside the seventh day for resting and reflection on the powers that made your blessing and rights available. Do not be counterfeit, in your not working, by employing others to work for you;

5. Respect your parents, good or bad, because they gave you life. If you do so, you'll come to enjoy life for a long time complete with prosperity;

6. Do not kill your body, mind, or spirit, or that of your fellow humans;

7. Respect the bonds of marriage;

8. Respect personal property rights, allowing others to be secure;

9. Do not lie, or even exchange lies and rumors about your fellow humans; and

10. Be happy for the possessions of others and do not desire their possessions as your own.

These ten rules are the development of a civil code which undoubtedly, whether by the hand of God or not, will ensure the existence of a peaceful society. More than any other law known, the ten commandments provide the foundation and the framework of societal and social respect.

Thanks to the study of these commandments, I have developed a formula for achieving a lasting social peace. This formula has, like the commandments, ten rules. They may not call for the same attention as the laws established by God for the nation of Israel but, if used consistently, they can aid in the establishment of order which results in peace.

Our world, especially America, is comprised of a large and diverse social body. It is disjointed by the lack of respect and tolerance for each other. Until now, the major focus of this book has been on race and gender. Small statements have clued the intelligent and discerning reader that the obstacles to social unity and harmony are larger. Bias, chauvinism, and prejudice are viruses waiting to infect anyone who has not immunized himself or herself against them.

The next ten chapters will discuss this formula. I call this formula the *Ten Commandments of Peace*. Understanding and applying them may not be the cure all to create social harmony, but it can certainly aid in the establishment of order that builds a harmonious society. These commandments are not for a specific body or community of people. They are for the individual. If individuals change, communities will change. If communities change, nations will change. If nations change, our world will change. The races can accept, live with, work with, play with, and enjoy each other. The sexes can complement each other. The generations can learn from each other. Religions can inspire common faith. Political party structures will die and give life to representational governments whose desires are to promote life, liberty, respect, and happiness to all.

These *Ten Commandments of Peace* should be taught, learned, and practiced immediately. Schools should promote them. Corporations should use them. Civic groups, dedicated to bettering our societies, should learn them. If you are a parent or guardian, you should know and live by them. As children learn to talk and walk, the values of these commandments should be instilled and this is best done by example.

These are the *Ten Commandments of Peace:*

1. Know and respect yourself;
2. Know and respect others;
3. Respect the laws of nature;
4. Appreciate the mutual design of humanity;
5. Appreciate the accomplishments and intelligence of others;
6. Be honest, never patronizing;
7. Avoid blanket statements;
8. Respect the right to dissent;
9. Always be willing to apologize and ready to forgive; and
10. Take time to rest;

Learn them, live them and share them . . .

9

Know and Respect Yourself

Rule #1 in the *Commandments of Peace*
If you don't who will?

I'm not certain who is responsible for saying it best. Was it the United States Army's recruitment line, "Be all that you can be," or was it the short children's story by Brad Sneed, "Lucky Russell?"

"Lucky Russell," is the story of a kitten named Russell, a farmer, his little daughter and a host of valuable animals found on the farm. Each of the animals had a specific task. These task, as perceived by Russell, gave his neighboring farm animals and friends a status of importance. They were needed. Each of his farm yard friends was somebody. In Russell's view he was a nobody. He was disrespected and disgraced. he was left, to his peril, to entertain the farmer's little girl. Day by day she would wheel him around the farm until they found their place in the shade of the cottonwood tree.

One morning the little girl put a bonnet on the kitty's head. this gave him the fidgets as she splashed milk into their cups for their imaginary tea party. For poor Russell this was embarrassing. As the farmer walked by, Russell ripped off the bonnet and dashed after him. Perhaps, the farmer would have something grown-up for him to do. He leaped and swatted at the farmer's feet. Noticing the kitty out of place the farmer returned the little fella back to the little girl.

On that evening Russell complained to his mother. He was tired of being treated like a baby. He needed an important job so the farmer would notice him too. He offered to help catch mice in the barn. She reminded him he was much too small to catch mice. "Be patient," she counseled him, "one day you'll be big enough to have a job on the farm." However Russell couldn't wait. He rushed off to the other farm animals.

He went to the horses, offering to help plow the fields He learned, after the big and strong horses neighed loudly, he was too small and weak. Even after standing on his paws and taking a deep breath, to look as big as possible, Russell agreed. Off to the hen he went only to be laughed at because, even though he tried, he couldn't lay eggs. Off to the cow he went hoping to give milk only to learn he needed an utter. Off to the dog he went where he nervously offered to protect the farm. The dog had a mean look and a low growl. Russell was cute and the only sound he could give was, "Meeeooowwwwwww." The dog was right so off to the sheep.

To the sheep he offered to make wool. But, his fur was not perfect for use in making the farmers clothes. To the pig he went offering to get fat hoping to be sold at the fair. But after seeing the slop the pig enjoyed, he politely walked on. He paid a visit to the goat. The goat trimmed the grass. This was easy. He could do this, so he thought. Sadly, after getting a mouth full and finding it hard to swallow, he decided that this was a job only a goat could do. Poor Russell headed for home. In the hayloft, without waiting for his mother to tuck him in, Russell closed his eyes and fell asleep.

The next morning, like every morning, the farmer's daughter wheeled Russell around the farm in the baby buggy. He looked out at the other farm animals doing their important jobs.

The goat was trimming the grass.
The pig was getting fat.
The sheep was making wool.
The dog was protecting the farm.

The cow was giving milk.

The hen was laying eggs.

The horse was pulling the farmer's plow.

His mother was catching mice.

And once again, the little girl and Russell were sipping milk under the big cottonwood tree when the farmer passed by. The farmer stopped and tipped his hat. "Good day to you, Miss. I see you have a fine playmate to share a pot of tea with."

The little girl smiled. Then the farmer picked up Russell. Stroking the kitty's ears he said, "And you little fella, are the luckiest critter on the farm." He then placed Russell in the little girl's arms and strolled back to the field.

The luckiest one? Russell pressed against the little girl and purred softly, then loudly. Russell had the most important job on the farm, even the farmer said so!

Who said it best? Was it the U.S. Army's slogan or the cute short story by Brad Sneed? Both address the issue of self-esteem.

But What Is Self-Esteem?

In my opinion, self-esteem is the energy from within that causes self-love or self-respect based on the confidence and satisfaction in one's self. It is knowing who you are, respecting who you are, believing in who you are, being proud of who you are, and building on who you are. It is about self-knowledge, self-worth, and becoming the best that you can be.

Charming, cuddly, cute little Russell had a problem. He was allowing himself to be defined from the outside in. It was his choice. He failed to realize that by playing with the little girl he helped the farmer be free to work.

Who are you? What is your level of self-esteem? Have you been distracted by the world around you? What kind of choices have you made? What are you becoming? Are you proud of who you are?

One of the oldest pieces of advice is:

"Know thy self." Knowing and understanding one's self is an activity that can only make one better.

The Highest Dive

During my days in college, I learned swimming was a good cardiovascular activity. Before coming to this knowledge, I had my share of those long and tasty boardwalk fries, deep-fried in peanut oil. I enjoyed steak and cheese subs, complete with fried onions and extra mayonnaise. I enjoyed the Godfather Deluxe Sicilian Pizza, with extra cheese. Sundaes with extra caramel, popcorn with extra butter. I need not tell you that all those extras taught me the real business about inflation. Like a balloon, I blew up. The extras cost more, and I weighed more. I had begun to walk around with what I developed as my extra self.

To balance this, each morning I would head for the pool. I would swim laps of the only strokes I could understand, the Breaststroke and the American crawl. Each day, while swimming, I found myself focused on the high dive.

It was back home in Annapolis, at the Truxtun Park pool, after not being permitted to swim at Jonas Greene, a little beach front along the Severn River, that I first began giving attention to the diving board. I was not a great swimmer. I understood just enough to get by. A couple of years earlier, my younger brothers, Clarence and Emory, and my older sister, Jackie, had begun swimming at the pool. By the time I made it, Emory and Jackie were already diving. Time after time, I was challenged to join in the diving fun. Mind games were played. The water below the high and low boards seemed to be 100 feet deep. My legs seemed only to be 2 feet long.

Somehow, when I began to swim, those legs with their feet planted in the river's sand, allowed me to appear as if I could swim. Back at Jonas Greene, in the dark green, algae- and seaweed-filled waters of the Severn, nobody could see my feet propelling me as I splashed along, with my arms doing this windmill thing. I got nowhere fast. Now and then, the undercurrent and roll of the cresting waves would leave me capsized, choking, and gasping for air. I finally got the hang of it. I was slow, but I could swim from one side of the pool to the other. But still, I was not about to dive. I tried to get my youngest brother, Clarence, to do it. He, too, was uncertain about diving. Finally, one day, on a dare, I climbed onto the low dive. I ran to the end and with eyes closed and breath held, I leaped. I don't know why I'm not dead. Maybe God has some work for me to do. I jumped as close as I could to the edge of the pool. I was hoping to catch the pool's wall, to avoid the disheartening embarrassment and disaster of drowning. People were yelling, whistles were being sounded by the lifeguards. I think and believe, I missed the wall by a fraction of an inch. About an inch more, and I would have jumped over the pool, missing the water entirely. Only embarrassment made me try again.

Let's face it, my swimming self-confidence was down. Not down, gone! But, how could it be gone if I never had it. You've got to have something to loose something. I did not loose my swimming confidence. I never had swimming confidence. My swimming abilities were not realized to the point that I could be satisfied. It was not until Oakwood College and, ironically, a lady named Faith, that I found help.

Each day, I would eye the high dive. Although terrified, I wondered what would it be like to jump from it. A number of college friends urged me to do so during the pool party. I gave logical excuses. "I'm feeling nauseous," I would tell them.

As time passed on, I became more confident. I enrolled in a swimming class and had my name placed on the Red Cross chart of those who swam a mile. Still no high dive; until one morning I was in the pool by myself. There was no Faith and no other lifeguard on duty. With childlike wonder in exploration, I went for the ladder. I climbed to the top then walked to the board's end. Then I froze! I looked at the water, it was deep and seemed deeper! But I, Donnell L. Harris, was going to conquer my fear, though not that day. Then I heard, "Jump!"

"Go ahead, jump!" she called. Faith had reentered the pool area. She was the lifeguard. She was the best lifeguard I had ever known. She insisted that I jump. I asked her to get the big pool hook ready. Her reply, "No! Just Do It!" Not wanting to humiliate and embarrass myself, I decided to retreat.

"Stop!" she yelled, "If you don't jump, you can not swim here anymore."

Was it to jump or give up a recreation that meant so much to me? I had to jump.

I stood at the diving board's end. I was hoping and praying that it would just happen. Dr. Norman Vincent Peale's, *Power of Positive Thinking* was not going to work for me now. I had to jump. I looked at the water and the strangest phenomenon took place. The longer I looked at the water, the further away it seemed. It had long passed the 100-foot depth of the water at the Truxtun Park pool. I was looking at the ocean's floor. Further, broader and deeper than any water I'd ever seen.

Finally, I jumped! During the time I spent in air, I know America went through three Presidents. I swam to the wall; I had conquered my greatest enemy! I climbed the ladder. I did it again; it was fun. I was not threatened by the pool, the height of the board or the lifeguard. My fear had existed because I did not know or respect myself. This unknown ability was hidden like a seed buried in the ground. It took root. Foolishly, without thinking, I nourished it. It grew. It blossomed. Its fruit was fear.

I could put down others who swam faster, harder, and more skillfully. I could put down the pool, the lifeguard and its management. I could laugh at and degrade others. I could find fault with beautifully executed dives by others, but that would not do anything but artificially bolster my self-esteem. Who was I? Was I the man who would deny the challenge of my own self? Did denying that challenge lessen the respect I had for myself. Trust me, that fateful day and that moment changed my life.

I learned facing one's self is difficult. Not facing one's self is foolish. Knowing one's self and suppressing the truth of one's self is disrespect to one's self. This disrespect is the worst kind. It limits a person's possibilities and capabilities by storing potential powers that develop the individual into the best that he or she can be.

The First Law

Who are you? Are you who you think you are? What makes you, you? Do you model your social environment? What is your environment? What does your environment teach you? The first law, in the *Ten Commandments of Peace* prompts such questions. Learning the answers may cause you to better respect yourself. I believe when we better respect ourselves, we better respect others. The more we respect others, the better are our chances of achieving a lasting peace.

The first law, "Know and Respect Yourself," is about personal accountability. Being personally accountable for your thoughts and actions is empowering. It is empowering because, when we waste time blaming others for our actions, we move steadily to a point of no change and stagnation. A negative environment may promote negative results in a person. Finding or identifying the negative influences ends in the realization that bits and pieces of negativity have influenced our personal habits. At this point, excuses are developed. "I do what I do because . . ."

When we become personally accountable for the thoughts and actions we use, it does not nullify the fact that we have been influenced by our environment. The influence still remains. Our personal accountability identifies our negative influences and seeks ways to eliminate them. To eliminate the effects of negative influences, we must come to terms with the hardest of enemies, ourselves. One must know one's self.

After learning of self, it is important to understand how the self aligns with society. Is society advanced, moving backward or left to evolve as it will, by our interaction. Let's face it, we all talk about a better world. But only we, by our interactions, can make a better world. After understanding the self, one must envision a better self. A self that lives to unite humanity, rather than divide it, should be the goal of any seeker of peace. If you can not honestly see yourself living to unite humanity, void the distractions of physical difference, you may find it difficult to respect yourself. Let's face it, if you can not respect yourself, it will be difficult to respect others.

Confidence Not Things Makes the Grade

Many people see themselves as secure because they have things. Those with lavish homes, fine automobiles, good food, powerful investments, and savings are usually no better off than those who may have adequate homes or no home, old vehicles or foot transit, little food or hunger, and no money. When it comes to social interaction, the lack of confidence affects the elite and the poverty-stricken. Perhaps this lack of confidence in the self stands behind the elite in our nation who legislate laws for their protection. Why else would the socially elite push for legislation to limit union activities, cap law suits against corporations, push for the construction of more prisons, promote the reduction of civil rights, move to eliminate affirmative action, push school voucher systems, eliminate gerrymandered districts designed to increase minority representation, or refuse to grant women, as all others, equality under the law? It is because leaders, bigoted and prejudiced men who have political pull and power, lack confidence in themselves. They try to favor themselves, and those who mirror them physically, due to lack of self-confidence. Not only does this lack of self-confidence appear in our leaders, it appears in us all in varying ways. For example, some older people who use canes and walkers may hurry to avoid delaying able-bodied people behind them. This lack of self-confidence deprives others of an opportunity to practice courtesy.

A courteous person is a self-reliant, strong, and self-respecting individual who is not afraid to positively interact with others who may be different. A courteous person will honestly examine the self. This person will come to know and take responsibility for the self. The responsible person will envision the self as it should be. Then as the target is set and ways are made to reach that goal, individual will enhance his or her self-respect.

Chance or Choice for Change

Journey back with me to the childhood stories of Mother Goose. Let me refamiliarize you with one story in particular the "Little Red Hen."

To make it short, the little red hen was strolling through the farm one day, when she happened upon some wheat. "Cutta', cut, cut," she ran off about the farm seeking help.

"Who," she asked of the fellow farm animals, "will help me cut the wheat?"

"Not I," was the chorus from her neighbors.

"Fine," she said, "then I'll cut it myself." This seeking of help for the cutting and threshing of the wheat continued throughout the bread-making process. The little red hen made a choice. She took a chance. Each time she found herself choosing to put out the effort. Each time she found herself completing the work. Finally, it was complete.

"Who" she asked, "will help me eat the bread?" Each reply, from each animal neighbor and friend, was "I will."

"No you won't!" She retorted. "When I came to you for help, you were lazy. I did the work. I and my little ones will receive the benefit of eating it."

The change was a step by step process. The process, which metamorphosized the common cereal grass, Gebus Triticum, was long and took effort. She, the little red hen, saw the simple wheat, but her vision did not stop there. Her vision allowed her to see what that wheat could become. She saw the loaf of bread. At once, with bold vision, she took a chance to solicit the aid of her brother and sister farm neighbors. It was her choice.

It was also her choice to move independently with self-determination and self-respect, knowing that it was harder but, in her power, to make a loaf of bread.

Our world is in desperate need of peace. We can not legislate it, mandate it, buy it, or sell it. We, as individuals, must see its need and envision it. We must take chances to request the aid of others to get there, but never give up of our efforts.

Trust me, when bread bakes, its aroma is delicious. It stimulates the salivary glands to pump, anticipating its taste. When the little red hen asked, "Who will help me eat the bread?" She did not have to look for or seek out volunteers. Her friends were right there. If you want peace, live for peace. Push for peace. Work for peace. Make peace happen. Soon the pleasant smell of peace will summon the attention of persons tired of conflict, tired of war, tired of death, tired of underhandedness, tired of destruction and division. They'll be there at your side. As we open the twenty-first century, let's open it working for peace.

How do you know yourself? Here are some questions that may get you started:

• Are you optimistic or pessimistic about the future?

• Are you a political individualist or a political partisan?

• Do you make frequent references to "they" when you speak of others who are different?

• Do you favor fairness to others, even if your slice of the social pie is reduced?

• Do you talk with others of different cultures or races, speaking of more than just the weather?

• Are you comfortable with opening your doors with welcome to someone of another culture or race?

• What types of shows or movies entertain you? How are people depicted in them who are different? Do they put down those who are different?

• When was the last time you told, listened to, or tolerated a bigot joke?

• How is diversity noticed and accepted in your workplace?

• Does your local religious body have a multicultural face?

• Is, or was, your school open to all?

• Do you have many friends who do not mirror you physically?

• Do you tolerate put-downs of other people?

• Are you easily offended?

• Do others, who are sexually, racially, economically, educationally, religiously, physically, and politically different, easily annoy you?

• Do others, especially of other races, call attention to their actions which are actions also displayed within your social or ethnic group?

• Are you cautious of people who are different?

• Do you speak or have opinions of others that are the result of ignorance?

• Can you name ten inventors, other than those who may mirror you, whose creativity you rely on each day?

Take time to consider these twenty questions. You may develop more. Honest answers may help you to better know yourself and the influences you have accepted from your environment. Be honest with the answers. Make certain your answers are consistent with peace. Any answer that nullifies another's right to life, or happiness, and encroaches upon his or her freedom is inconsistent with peace. If you respect yourself, you must be honest with yourself. You will come to know yourself. You will gain confidence in yourself. You will build in yourself an ambassador of peace.

Law Number One—Know and Respect Yourself

10

Know and Respect Others

Rule #2 in the *Commandments of Peace*

What is the cause of darker skin? What causes a baby to be born of a different nationality? Why are there two genders? Why are there so many religious thoughts and teachings? Why is there the large gap between rich and poor? Why do some amass great educational backgrounds? Why are others lacking the foundation or the economic means for the attainment of a formal education seen as ignorant? What does cause homosexuality? Why are some people born physically disabled?

The question "why" is not as important as how we react. In America, many have formed or joined bigoted clubs and prejudiced groups of hatred. Today, how we react to our nation and world has caused animosities, some resulting in violence. Land, sea, and air travel have been reduced to luck, as terrorism waits to expose its evil face. Families have been torn apart, communities fragmented. The group of people supporting the creed of humanity is eroding. The words of Rodney King are resonating, daily challenging us: "Can we all just get along?"

Trading Places

I can not recall how old I was. I know I was in elementary school. I remember it was summer. I was in the front yard playing with my bike. A couple of days before, near the same area, I was stung by a bee that made its home in a nest, in the Lilac bush, at the corner of the yard. The entire community of bees that I knew of took up residence there. I remember doing the traditional dance of terror, as only a child could do. With the ego I've got today, I look back on that bee sting. It was on my head just above my ear. I guess that was the first time I suffered from a swollen head. I believe, after that day, my ego was reduced and made semiresponsible. Two days after my bee assault, I was at play. A car pulled up to the mail box and the driver called for me.

"Hello kid, cana' you help a' mae'?"

To me it was funny. He was funny. He was driving a yellow taxi. He looked like someone on the television with his thin mustache and curly black hair. His skin was White but he seemed friendly.

"Hurry," he said, with his two way radio blasting in the background.

"I'ma looking for de' ah'; one-a' two-a' Dor'sa Road-a'."

I got a good laugh, but I listened close. I lived on Dorsey Drive, maybe fifty feet outside the city line. In the city was an avenue named Dorsey. Maybe he had confused the two. Apparently he was having difficulties understanding his map. Obviously he was having a language problem. Later, I had my own language problem.

I was then 19. I had completed my first year of college and was somewhere in Japan. I was between Hiroshima and Tokyo. I had gone there to teach conversational English and scout out persons willing to become Christian. I was stationed in Osaka. I had just finished meeting on a little island near the southern tip of Japan's largest island, Honshu. Back on the mainland, I had taken a ride home to Osaka. I was by myself on the Shinkansen, known to us as the "Bullet Train."

While on the train, I spoke with many people. I was somewhat, as one Japanese boy said, "a novelty." It was rare to see men of African descent in that country. If an American of African descent was seen in Japan, it was usually around

American military bases, on television, or in the big cities of Tokyo and its suburbs.

Back home, I was defined as a minority. I really wasn't, though. Only when I related publicly to the majority in common areas such as stores, schools, or hospitals was I a minority. Certain people in society made certain that fact was driven home. In reality, I was in the majority. My community was completely African-American until the young White couple moved in two doors down. I was a member of a Black church and the only fire known to its congregation was spiritual. It was classified as Christian but many of its members and leaders practiced separatism. More than a few practiced hate. Not only was this evident racially but socially, politically and religiously, as well.

When I got my haircut, I went to barbers whose clientele were Black and male. Only once at Chamber's barber shop do I recall seeing a White customer. Who knows, he could have been Black. Some Blacks that I knew could pass for White. So I'm not sure, but I am confident that I was a member of the majority within my predominant social world. I'm also certain it was a minority, in the overall majority of the major racial type, that willingly, without compassion, or sensitivity, caused stress in my majority.

In Japan, I was absolutely and unquestionably a minority. My skin was dark, my hair thick and tightly curled. For the first time, I was tall. My feet were huge. My voice was deep. For the first time, I was a real minority.

After boarding the train and taking pictures, with friendly people who were strangely hospitable and nice, I sat in my seat. Like a warm and humid summer Sunday, I was nestled and cradled in the large comfortable cushions. The sound of travel and the long exciting day had lulled me off to sleep. When I awoke, we were just leaving another stop on a long trip. Something was announced and I had no idea what it was. I could not speak Japanese. I knew where I was. I was on the train but I was lost! Had my stop been called? Was this my stop? How long did I sleep?

Frantically, I jumped from my seat. I scurried through the aisles seeking someone who spoke English. I had unbelievable hellos.

"Do you Speak English," I would ask.

"Yes," was the usual reply. "How do you do?" was the only English most people could speak, but it was said with a smile.

While I was sleeping, I had seemingly entered the Twilight Zone. In this area, in this environment, I had traded places. I was now the odd man out that I found so amusing in my youth. I had exchanged places with the lost and confused taxi driver. Only now it was not as funny. "Help!" I urgently called to a group of people. "Help!"

I found help. I was told I had passed my stop. I was headed who knows where. A kind man in a black turtleneck shirt put me on the right track.

Each day millions cry out for help. We only hear a few, if we hear any. Their cries come in all forms. "Help!" is the cry of the high school graduate hoping to further his or her education. "Help!" is the cry of the young female seeking opportunity in the corporate world, not a date. "Help!" is the snivel of a kid whose teary eyes are beholding the promise granted athletes as they seek scholarships and hunt opportunity. "Help!" cry homeless children, unsheltered by no fault of their own. "Help me!" is the moan of the alcoholic and the drug addict reaching for that rail of sobriety.

"Help! Help! Help!" is echoed by displaced workers as the corporate world shrinks to ensure their company's profits. "Help!" is the cry of souls seeking liberty and peace. High above the Lady's torch standing in New York harbor, over the hills of the Appalachians, deep into the gaps and crevices of the Grand Canyon, lining the shores of the mighty Mississippi, and over the winding roads clashing against America's West Coast, people need help.

"Help!" is the cry of persons locked out by their lack of representation in the political process. "Help" is the cry of homosexuals, not seeking Christian status but legal fairness and respect in their family unions, as they seek rights afforded to heterosexual marriages.

"Help, I'm lost!" is the cry of young people as they turn to their churches only to witness the division organized religion has created in the human family. Young people are not stupid. They understand the hypocrisy of the profiteers whose only goal is money. They see a racially united heaven, but find great difficulties understanding our racially disunited earth. "Help" is a constant call by many, maybe not always as extreme. But, whether the case is extreme or not, the only way to understand the call is to identify the caller.

Identifying the caller does not mean identifying *with* the caller. It may sound as if I am leading you to believe in order for the rich to understand the poverty stricken, the rich must rid themselves of their wealth. This would be absurd. However, time taken to understand the plight of those who are different is commendable because understanding them leads one to know them. Knowing them requires one to respect them.

The variables here, in the preceding example, are rich and poor. Change them by race, gender, educational background, religious or political leanings, sexual orientation, age or anything else that divides us. You will still find understanding people requires you to know people. Knowing people allows you to respect them.

Understanding people does not require agreement. Understanding simply means mentally grasping their ideologies then showing tolerance. A good example is the Jew and the Christian. Most observers and devotees of Judaism await the coming of an Anointed one, Christ, the Messiah. Most Christians believe the Anointed one, Christ, the Messiah has come, gone, and is coming again. Understanding one another's religions is a short step in trading mindsets.

The same if true of race, gender, educational background, political ideology, sexual orientation, age, or anything else. Taking time to understand the other's perspective requires not changing but trading mental places.

More Than a Game for Kids

When I was a kid I played the role of my father. I put on his suit coat and his shoes. I slid around the room in my deepest, roughest, manliest voice. I gave the orders. "Cook the food! Clean the House! I'm going to work!" The game was fun.

Like most children I was a teacher, minister, fireman, policeman, doctor, lawyer, judge, construction worker, telephone man, Indian, cowboy, baseball player, as well as a host of other exciting characters. Like most kids, I was role playing, and having fun, too. But role playing is more than a child's game. It is a game that we adults can learn from.

Let us use this example. A child takes a cookie and is caught by a parent. Quickly, the child looks into the parent's face. With warp speed, the parent is photographed. This picture is quickly processed and developed into the child's mind for role play. While mentally in the role of the parent, the child, with warp speed, examines the body language, analyzes the tone of voice, scrutinizes the word usage and facial expressions. After processing this information the child just as quickly determines whether it is best to laugh, cry, look sorry, put up a fight, or run. It is not necessary that the child becomes a parent to understand a parent. Understanding the parent requires focus and attention. It allows the child to know the parent. Adults understanding this process can serve well the second law of peace. Understanding others requires knowing others.

How do others live, eat, work, worship, sleep, etc.? Knowing others begins with knowing self. How do you live, eat, work, worship, sleep, etc.? Knowing yourself is knowing the answers. Knowing the answers leads us to understanding what we do. No natural law causes us to operate as we do. The way we operate is by choice based on personal experiences. If we take the time to analyze our daily interactions, it will become clear how important role playing is.

By role play, children learn what adults are thinking and how to better please them. They learn how to interact with other children. They learn to avoid fights. They learn how to make and keep friends. Could there be a better foundation for diplomacy?

Parents and guardians of children, including teachers and other professionals catering to the child, by role play, learn how to best serve and protect the child. Employees, good and bad, learn to conform by role play. Their role play limits the distance they can go without bringing forth negative reactions and sanctions. Many employers see role playing as foolish and may feel secure by their position and authority. However, the employer who systematically ignores the employee and fails to understand the employee by role play may create a hostile work environment, lower morale, and produce a high turn-over rate.

We role play when we love or feel sorry for others. Our role playing is about learning to see through the eyes of another. Role playing is about understanding. Understanding is about knowing. Knowing and respecting others is about making our world a more tolerant and loving place. Having a more tolerant and loving world is about having a world at peace.

Judge Ye Not

Many times, when we judge others and their motives, we become suspicious. We are suspicious because our judgments of others are based not on their lives and experiences but our understanding of others played by ourselves. It is our lives and our experiences, projected onto others, that determine the mindset of people we hardly know.

Earlier in this book, I told you of my work in the District of Columbia and its suburbs. It was there I witnessed, first-hand, the deplorable living conditions of a number of citizens. Some lived in homes which were not abandoned but windows boarded up due to thrown items, rocks, and bullets from ignorantly selfish people who just did not care. Some apartments were furnished with only blankets, having communal hallways with lights blown out, knocked out, or shot out.

It was here that the stench of aged human urine, from drunkards hanging out in these areas conveniently relieving themselves, left an unforgettably offensive, odorous impression. No wonder why some, when left with the choice of crime, are enticed. In this picture, if the criminal is caught and sentenced to time isolated from society, prison becomes a step up. If they are not caught, the rewards of their misdeeds are a step up. Spending time knowing the people in these areas, rather than studying them, will be a benefit to the whole society. Now, I do not suggest this is the end result of the inner city residents. I do not suggest only people of the inner city are doomed to this end. Suburbia, too, grapples with an assortment of problems.

In suburbia, children having babies, drugs, alcohol, theft, suicide, murder, and divorce, hover as dark and unnoticed clouds. Knowing the people there, rather than studying them, will also benefit society. Bigots, prejudiced by a seemingly innate hatred of people superficially different than themselves, fill the streets of the cities and country alike. We judge the intent of others from another race, national origin, sex, religion, political viewpoint, age, economic standard, or educational background, without taking the time or chance to know them. We should remember not to judge others, but to know and respect them.

Law Number One—Know and Respect Yourself

Law Number Two—Know and Respect Others

11

Respect the Laws of Nature

Rule #3 in the *Commandments of Peace*

My uncle once shared this anecdote:

"There was a man who constantly complained of having no shoes. One day he walked around a corner and met another man who had no feet."

There are some things in this world you can do nothing about. On the other hand, there are other things in this world you can do something about. My uncle's lesson was about contentment. Knowing when to be content with things as they are makes a difference.

Do you know or have you prayed the serenity prayer?

"God grant me the serenity
to accept the things I can not change,
the courage to change the things I can
and the wisdom to know the difference."

This prayer, in itself, is wisdom. Let it be certain in your mind, there are some things you can do something about. Let it be equally clear, there are some things you can do nothing about. Sometimes all you can do is accept the situation.

Do you remember the Jackson 5? Do you remember the songs, "A-B-C As Easy As 1-2-3," "You Better Stop, the Love You Save May Be Your Own," and, "Who can forget Ben?" The star of the group was a little boy named Michael.

Their star singer is all grown up now. They're gone and he's gone, or is he? The Michael Jackson we see today is in a new, physically enhanced, and chemically altered form. Of him, my brother-in-law, a high school student, said to me, "Michael Jackson is the only person I know who was born a little Black boy and grew up to be a little White girl."

His nose, face, skin, his hair, his voice are all different. Even with the renovations, chemical and physical alterations, he is still no more than the talented and much loved singer, Michael Jackson. Recent events and charges may have diminished his name and status, but he is still the soul held tight in the body to which he was born.

Millions upon millions of dollars are spent yearly by insecure people, physically dissatisfied with themselves. They possess an inadequate self-image and low self-esteem. People the world over, especially in America, have paid to have their lips enlarged or reduced, noses altered, breasts reduced, breasts enlarged with dangerous silicone implants, shapes altered, liposuctioned and undergone sex changes. But whatever we do to enhance, recreate, or rebuild our bodies, we can not escape the soul, the conscience or the body we were given at birth.

Foolishly, we press and strive against nature. Humanity and the natural effects of nature are in constant competition, and conflict in a contest where the combative laws of nature have always and will always win. Change your hair color, straighten your teeth, color your eyes with the application of contact lenses, talk differently, loose weight, gain weight, get high, get sober, you were, still are and will be you. Maybe you are more or maybe less comfortable with yourself but you can not escape the person you are. You are you, and until you cease to exist, you will forever be you. So respect the laws of nature and be the best that you can be.

What Are the Laws of Nature?

Before answering this question one should know and understand nature. Nature, most simply put, is the universally

creative and controlling force that defines the character and
the basic constitution of every form of breathless matter and
breathing life forms known and unknown, seen and unseen
by humanity. Nature is the inanimate force that separates the
sandy beach from rock on a mountain's peak. Nature is the
inanimate paintbrush that strokes on the colors, painting leaves
and flowers, man and animal. It is nature that carves the path
of waters high upon mountains to travel to rivers and streams
below and leads them to the seas and oceans. It is nature that
gravitationally pulls down from up. It stirs the composition of
the seed and presses against the inner-seed wall, cracking,
breaking, grabbing, and rooting into the soil while cosmically
reaching beyond its home up towards the sun to copy and
reproduce its own again and again. Mankind can alter, but
never produce life. Nature holds the patent on that secret.

It is nature, not human will, that floats the ship, raises the
plane. Many would define these as the inventions of man.
They are, but these inventions are only mechanical and used
to harness and trap the forces of nature. At times, the powers
of nature are too great and the ship sinks, or the plane falls.

Nature has tied into the earth, the wind, the sun, the
waters, forces which can be used, but never altered. While the
creative genius of a man may enhance or alter the color of a
rose, he cannot produce, design, or create a living, growing
rose. While man can alter the earth by the destructive forces
of warfare, he cannot produce, design, or create earth. The
abilities of mankind are limited by natural law. As humans,
we push, strive, and contend with the laws of nature. We do
this most forcefully against ourselves. God is the author of
natural law. We can work against it, speak against it, even
protest it, but we will only be reminded, we are no match for
it.

One of the worst habits, in the human family, is our
battle against the natural law. When humans were created,
nature was given the authority to alter, as necessary, the forms.
In chapter five, I called this adaptive evolution. Through this
process, humanity has developed into a rainbow of human
colors and an assortment of shapes, sizes, and measurable

ranges of intelligence. These differences are superficial.

We tend to focus on our superficial differences and conclude our likes and dislikes. Quickly, before we come to terms allowing us knowledge of self, we determine and conclude our likes and dislikes of others. No matter how complex, before we begin to understand ourselves, we claim to understand others. Our beliefs and understanding of others is our social understanding. Understanding is knowledge. This knowledge is uneven and flawed. Upon it is built our prejudices and biases on the figurative and literal draw from nature's law alone. The literal draw of nature's law is the natural artistry that sketches and colors us differently. The figurative draw, from nature's law, is our selection from the card deck of difference. The laws of nature are peculiar, at times humorous, but always unpredictable. Those who do not understand this make stupid errors.

Consider this, the person who prays the serenity prayer is undoubtedly already wise. Also, when the laws of nature are understood and respected, the stupid errors we make will be corrected. We can erect sails to harness the power of the wind. By this combination, we are forced east or west, but we can not control the wind. We can alter or plant the seed, but we cannot create it. Mechanically, we can rush across the surface of the earth. We can also soar through the heavens. Electronically, we can communicate within an extended but limited area of the universe via satellite. With all this, in us, is found no match for the infinite nature of heavens or earth.

> God grant us all the serenity to
> accept the things we cannot change.
> Give us the courage to change the things we can.
> Then grant us the wisdom to know the difference.

A syllogism is a subtle but crafty argument of deductive reasoning. This deductive reasoning is usually an argumentative scheme consisting of a major premise, a minor premise and a conclusion. The conclusions are often faulty because they depend overwhelmingly on inference. Well, what is an inference?

An inference is a theory supported by the determination that a proposition, statement, or judgment is sound and true based on a former proposition, statement, or judgment which is known or simply believed to be true.

Syllogisms and inferences may at times be true. More often the conclusions are indicative of isolated models used to broadbrush variables which are similar to the example. Sometimes the conclusions are true and sometimes the conclusions are false.

Example: "Birds of a feather flock together."

While this statement may apply to a squadron of geese flying high above in their v-formation it is not transferable to all living matter that willfully finds itself in communion with living matters of physical difference. A member of the Ku Klux Klan who surrounds himself or herself with friends and acquaintances who agree with them are covered by the foregoing statement of "birds of a feather flock together." But no individual is a duplicate of those who surround him or her; this is the pinnacle and premise behind Christianity.

The bird was Jesus. He was pure, kind, and true. He represented the best humanity had to offer. Jesus was full to capacity and overflowing with love, compassion, joy, peace, patience, kindness, goodness, faithfulness, gentleness, and self-control. However, His circle of admires did not reflect Him. Jesus was the human progeny of a known adulterer and murderer. In His lineage, both maternal and paternal (by adoption), one finds liars, bigots, racist, faithless, restless, unkind and quick tempered individuals some who lacked self-control. If the statement, "Birds of a feather flock together," were always true, those who follow the teachings of Christ would be perfect. Christ was an individual who practiced individuality. He respected His community and His world. Many, who were unlike Him were drawn to him. The flock consisted of a multitude of kinds of people.

Logic can be faulty. Many times we fall prey to legends and popular myths. The conclusions drawn from legends and myths override natural laws and take on the form of interactive law. It is by this law we interact with one another. It is by this law that the viruses of bigotry and hate are injected, rendering the host prejudiced. The prejudiced mind is the mind that is directed not by experience but rather the inferential laws of logic.

Here's another example:

Fact #1: Mutsuhiro is Japanese.

+   Fact #2: Mutsuhiro is short.

= Syllogistic Inference: Since Mutsuhiro is short and Japanese therefore all Japanese are short.

How silly! First, what is short? Secondly, Mutsuhiro is short by what comparison? While on average, it may be rare to see Japanese person standing 6 feet tall, it is a fact that some Japanese measure 6'5" and more. The average American male measures a little over 5 and a half feet tall. The average American male pales remarkably in comparison to some basketball greats like Shaq O'Neil, Dennis Rodman, or George Murasen who stands 7 feet 7 inches tall. Japanese may be short in comparison to the average American, but in his community, Mutsuhiro may be a giant.

Here is a short list of categories that contains a number of prejudiced blanket statements believed by many to be true. These statements may echo an element of truth, but are preposterous. They are not consistent with reality.

On American Political Parties...

Democrats are liberal and immoral.
Republicans are conservative and Christian.
Democrats lack national pride.
Republicans are concerned and care for the nation.
Libertarians are leftist anarchist.
All politicians are crooks.

On Nationalities and Origins...

Germans are evil, racially polarized, and hate mongers.
Italians are prone to racketeering and mob activity.
Greeks make good, passionate lovers.
Jews are money hungry, frugal, and cheap.

Polishmen lack intelligence.
Africans are uncivilized and poor.
Russians hate Americans and want war.
Mideasterners are evil, sinister, and quick tempered.

On the races . . .

Hispanics are dirty, trashy, and lazy.
Black men are full of sexual energy.
White girls who date Black men are sluts.
Interracial marriages don't last.
Orientals are highly intelligent.
Black kids are inclined to use crack.
White kids are predispositioned to over-indulge in alcohol.
Blacks have rhythm.
Whites can't dance.
Indians are superstitious.

On the sexes . . .

Single women love cats.
Females are weak and lack leadership.
Women are bad drivers.
Real men are strong and masculine.
Men are dogs.
Men make the best leaders.
Lesbians were abused by male authority figures.
Female tennis players are lesbians.
Gays are highly talented and creative.
Men who are bank tellers and waiters are wimps.
Effeminate men are gay.
Women with short haircuts are lesbians.

On people in general or just in the head . . .

Blondes are silly, empty headed, easy, and promiscuous.
Redheads are outgoing and fun.
Weathermen have bald heads.
All skinheads are evil.
Dittoheads are intelligent.
Rich people lack compassion.

Poor people want handouts.
Deaf people are stupid.
Blind people cannot hear.
Rich people are happy.
Poor people are miserable.
Fat people are lazy.
Old people are frail, weak, and ignorant.
Old people are narrow-minded.

On religious faiths and customs . . .

Christians are dogmatic, narrow minded, and intolerant.
Christian people are Christ-like.
Catholics are not Christian.
Catholic priests molest little boys.
Catholics worship the Pope.
Seventh-Day Adventists don't eat meat.
Baptists are rowdy fundamentalists.
Charismatics are fanatical.
Mormons are bigamists.
Jehovah's Witnesses are fanatics.
Preachers steal money.
Ministers use the Bible to oppress people.
Muslims teach and practice hate.
Jews hate Christians.
Unitarian Universalists are atheists.

These faulty generalizations are all wrong. There are
countless others. This is rude, insensitive, and wrong. No
blanket statement covers an entire group of people. If you
belong to a group that practices generalization, if by race,
religion, politics, education, wealth, sex, or whatever, leave
them alone. Make a decision. Come out! If you have taken
time to read this book, you are better than that.

Heal your communities. Heal your nations. Heal your
world. In the beautifully sung words of Michael Jackson and
a chorus of friends we hear:

> There's a place in your heart
> And I know that it is love.

And this place could be much
Brighter than tomorrow.
And if you really try
You'll find there's no need to cry.
In this place you'll feel
There's no hurt or sorrow.

There are ways to get there.
If you care enough for the living,
Make a little space,
Make a better place.

Heal the world
Make it a better place
For you and for me,
And the entire human race.
There are people dying
If you care enough for the living
Make a better place
For you and for me.

The Human Laws

There are all sorts of laws. Laws are bodies of official rules and regulations, used to govern a society, and to regulate and control the behavior of its members. Laws are usually good. They contribute to safety as demonstrated by the red, yellow, and green traffic signal. Respecting and obeying traffic signals saves lives. However, at times, laws can be poisonous and damning to the society. When this occurs, I refer to it as negative law.

Negative law is established law based on popular and public opinion. It is a law that is usually based on custom and tradition. Negative law is usually biased law, in which, one group may subdue or usurp another. This use of law can only result from human law. Human laws are those laws established by humans for altruistic purposes, or for selfish gain, by which one group may achieve a head start over another. When this occurs, which it frequently does in human law, disrespect grows. The skin of humanity is torn and an open sore festers.

Sooner or later, those oppressed by human law will stand and rebel. There is no force mightier than natural law. Natural law is impressed upon the soul of humanity. This is why you may kill the dreamer, but if a dream is noble, you will never kill the dream.

Today, the lack of respect for the laws of nature has become an obstacle to peace. For example, because we are more in tune with the senses of sight, hearing, smell, taste, and touch, we can understand and make exceptions for those born without sight or hearing. We allow for those born without certain extremities like hands, feet, legs, and arms. Compassion is usually shown to the disabled. But how can we justify our hatred and preoccupation with gays?

Respecting the laws of nature means respecting and appreciating the variations it offers. This respect and appreciation requires love. This love can only be universally and divinely inspired. This love is known to be patient and kind. This love is never jealous, boastful, or proud. This love is not rude or selfish. It is never quick to anger. This love is positive love. Its positive forces dampen the negativities and wrongs launched against it. This love is real love. Real love is not tolerant of or happy with evil. Real love seeks truth. Real love patiently accepts all things and respects our differences. It forever trusts, always hopes, and is perpetually strong. Real love never ends. This love can only be unfolded in the person who respects the laws of nature.

Human laws are faulty based on our well-intended but biased thoughts. Inferential laws are silly, cheap, foolish, and an insult to human intelligence. Blanket statements, generalities and inferences are no more than stereotypes and a failure in the test of consistency.

The laws of Nature are consistent and trustful. Men carry sperm. Women carry eggs. Oak trees do not come from apple trees. Gravity pulls water, delivering it from up to down. Each second of life we turn a second older, never younger. Finally, by nature's choice, we are delivered into bodies shaped, formed, and colored, by nature. Respect its choice. Respect the laws of nature.

    Law Number One—Know and Respect Yourself

    Law Number Two—Know and Respect Others

    Law Number Three—Respect the Laws of Nature

12

Appreciate the Mutual Design of Humanity

Rule #4 in the *Commandments of Peace*

My granddaddy never finished elementary school. Back in the early 1900s, it was unpopular for the descendants of slaves to spend time getting a formal education. No credentials for reading, writing, and arithmetic were usually earned. Granddad adhered to the social standards. Even though he was paid, his status in American society was still one of slave. If tired or sick, he still had to rise before dawn to work. He had no choice. He lived on his employer's property, he farmed on their land, and drank from their streams. To his employer's sons and daughters, many years his junior, he was a "boy."

He was a man designated by some a boy. He married a woman some disrespectfully called a gal. To that so-called boy and gal were born two sons and a daughter. Natural law would instill in him a thirst for knowledge, a drive for growth, and he would establish himself as a husband and father. Natural law placed deep within his mind, a dream to watch his children grow and expand, establishing themselves as productive and respected members of a society bent on oppression. However, in his thirst, his drive, his dream, he would find them all suppressed, vaulted deep within a heart, haunted by fear. Could his sons be doctors, dedicated to the brotherhood of healing? Could his daughter be a lawyer, pursuing justice for all? Could she stand in courtrooms challenging the nation's constitution and laws?

How would he ever afford to provide clothes for his family, food for their stomachs, a roof for shelter, and walls for their safety? His choice was a choice of implied limitation. He was limited, not by law but, by mores and the teaching and examples of selfish men and women whose only claim to superiority was the color of their skin.

Even when granddaddy was told that his young, strong, and able-bodied sons should not go to school, rather help him in the fields, he insisted on their completing high school. In 1941, when his sons graduated, they carried the social status equivalent to today's college graduates. There were very few college grads per capita in that year, and even fewer of African-American descent.

Today, I am proud of my father, uncle, and aunt. Although they may have smoked, drank, or sworn, I have never seen them do that. Today, with the high percentages of marriages ending in divorce, my grandfather can boast of his children, grandchildren, and great-grandchildren, not one divorce. I, along with my many cousins, have learned to respect the family unit. Of the many degrees offered and conferred each year in sociology, and the certifications in marital counseling, few American families have such a good record.

Granddad the Scholar

Our nation's debt is a catastrophe, only to be placed upon the backs of our generations to come. With all the economists, mathematicians, and accountants in the U.S., you would think America could control and limit its deficit. Check the record. Democrats, Republicans, Libertarians, Perotites, and Independents have argued and fought with no honest end to our national debt in sight.

Granddaddy taught me years ago to look out for my economic future. "Donny," he said, "just because you've got a dollar don't mean you spend it. You'd better learn to spend some and save some. Always live within your means."

Granddaddy taught me to stand for what is right. "Donny," he said, "everything legal ain't fair, and if it ain't fair, it hadn't ought to be legal." Granddaddy taught me to look out for others. Now, sometimes I took his advice a little too far. I remember I was at college, earning my bachelor's degree. During a winter's break, I stayed on campus. I worked, and worked hard. Because my car was broken, many days I walked for miles to and from work. I was usually looking out for others. If I was motivated to fix the car, it was usually to help someone else. This kept me broke. But I was always able to pay my bills. When I did decide to fix the car, I had the money to do it.

Now a special deal was made between the vice president of student affairs and myself. I could stay on campus, at a reduced rate, in order to keep my job which was off-campus. However, I did not want to purchase a meal plan. The college food, in my opinion, was not good. Others may have loved it, but it was nothing in comparison to what I had learned to appreciate. Well, the vice president talked me into taking a few meal tickets. If I needed to, I would have food to eat. He was a great guy. I found him to be a Christian, until one day I spoke with some friends. I told them how kind the V.P. had been to me. A couple of them shared stories about why they couldn't go home. Their families wanted to be rid of them. You see, I was learning something new. Homosexuality and the societal hatred and venomous attitudes towards it. I sent some guys who were known homosexuals to the V.P. for help. I already knew of his hatred and bigoted comments towards them. I guess it was because he was Christian. That's the excuse most people use to hide their prejudice and intolerance. Some way I learned and still believe it is a Christian's call, and duty to show love, respect, charity, courtesy, and patience to all. Man or woman no matter what the exterior may present, everybody is somebody, and that in itself is deserving of respect. When a few returned from the V.P.'s office with the news, I optimistically instructed them not to worry. My rent was paid and they were welcome, if needed, to share my lodging.

Now and then, I used my money to help feed people. Not only on campus, but off campus as well. It was known only to those I aided that I would sit down and eat with some of the vilest rejects of society. But little did they know, I was learning the stories behind faces. Each face has a story. Each heart has a song. Whether that song was happy or sad depended on that person's own personal experience. My job was to see that the person's experience was a happy and worthwhile one, while in company with me.

One day, I was returning to campus, in my repaired, but still broken car. I thought, to myself, I do a lot to help others. I looked out at the new and pretty cars. I looked at the lovely homes. I thought of the clothes I wore, many purchased from second hand stores. I'm a nice guy. I can't find a date. I work, sleep, and if I get the chance, I eat. I had usually put others first. What did I get out of the deal? Nothing! Nothing! *Nothing,* so I thought.

I came up with the brainiest scheme. I had helped to feed others out of my pocket. I had gone to some school officials asking that the leftovers from the cafeteria be shared with the needy, only to be refused. My scheme was this: make my money more efficient.

The V.P. who I was losing respect for fast, had given me meal tickets. If I copied, designed, and reproduced them, I could spend a little money and feed a lot, "spend some, save some." Granddad might be proud. I did it. I copied and distributed the tickets. I was so childishly proud, I gave some to the not-so-needy. I was too stupid to use them myself. I had a job! I was paid! I had money!

I wish I had known that all good deeds "ain't" good. It is not good to watch a neighbor get robbed and do nothing other than mind your business. It is not good to watch a man beat his wife and when he turns to you for solace say, "I understand." It is not good to stand by and watch someone get railroaded, in the name of progress, only to turn a head in ignorance. It is not good to help someone, while hurting another, no matter how mighty the injured party may be. My father, my grandfather, and a host of other relatives and friends taught me better. But, let it be known, if we see someone being denied, unnecessarily, their natural rights to life, liberty, and pursuit of happiness we must do all we can give to aid. We must help to remove obstacles and barriers. We must fight for fairness and justice. We must strive always for the betterment of humanity. It is our world. It is on loan to make it a better place.

Granddaddy may not have gone far, but as my professor he has taught me a great deal. Sure, I've failed an exam here and maybe a few there. But in general, I've been a good student.

Granddaddy was also my agricultural expert. At a very young age, he taught me how to plant bulbs and seeds. Some of the plantings were for sustenance, others were for beauty. In boxes, pots, and gardens alike, he taught me to respect the conservation and cultivation of plants. One of the great lessons in learning this was learning to appreciate variety. I further learned the appreciation of human variety.

In variety is beauty. Someone said, "beauty is skin deep." This statement is overused and, when dealing with the whole of life, false. Beauty is deep. It is much deeper than skin. Real beauty is found in the seed. As the seed develops, it raises to blossom beauty that blesses the eye. Nature has within its bag of gifts, the endowment of beauty. It is freely handed over to us, for our appreciation. It is found in variety . If God never intended variety, we all would have been born duplicates of our parentage, Adam and Eve. Variety is the mutual design of humanity and we must learn to appreciate it.

Why Should We?

Most theists, believe it was God who created the universe. The opening line to the book of Genesis, reads, "In the beginning God created the heavens and the earth." If this statement is true, it could further be suggested, if God did not intend our world to develop variety, God would have created everything the same.

God created humans, and in the seed of humanity was an ever-changing ever-adapting combination which would safeguard its survival. The only real and unchangeable ways we are alike is in our conception by the union of the sperm and egg and the close of our living journey as earthly human inhabitants.

It was the artistic and creative force that set into motion variety. Variety is the design of nature. We have scientifically learned to alter some forms of life. Naturally and unnaturally, we have altered the color, shape, and size of a rose. Today the rose family contains more than 107 genera and more than 3100 species. I call that variety. But, a rose is still a rose, and its beauty and fragrance is inviting to the soul captured by love.

The animal and plant kingdoms are broken into phylum or primary divisions of the kingdoms. On this level, man and fish share a commonality. Later, the phylum are separated into classes. In the class, man and fish are separated. Humans are warm blooded mammals who produce milk to feed their young. On this level, mankind shares a commonality with cats and dogs. The classes are then separated into orders. In this order, we humans are primates upright walkers, sharing a commonality with the ape family. The monkeys, gorillas, orangutans, gibbons, and chimpanzees are separated from humans in every way when it comes to the order division of families. It is here that you and I share a commonality. Here we are only known as *homo sapiens*. We have an intellectual ability reaching far beyond all life forms. We control life by our choices.

Only we are *homo sapiens*. We are male and female. We have large brains, in comparison to any other living matter. We can operate on instinct and learning alike. We have the intellectual capacity to reach far beyond any other earthly like form. We can reach deep into the universe. We control life by our collective and personal choices.

Even with this, the human family is broken into genera. Here we differ only superficially by race. Here the mutual design of humanity takes on color. Here we are painted in an array of hues and shades. Again, we are broken down. This is the last taxonomic grouping. It is the species. Here we become three dimensional.

Depending on the experiences and diets of a given community, we take on height and weight which is later photocopied onto the genetic structure by way of deoxyribonucleic acid (DNA). It is here that hereditary codes are stamped to be duplicated upon the progeny. Hereditarily, we display pictures of our heritage. Each face has a story. It speaks of connections, both by nature and choice. Naturally we are old, young, male, female, and colored by race. But by choice, we are theist and atheist. We are Jews and Gentiles. We are Protestants and Catholics. By choice we are political, educated, rich, and poor. Somehow our differences are all part of our creator's plan creating diversity.

Mutually, we have received a natural and chosen design. Humanity is not limited by the laws of nature, but naturally allowed to grow and expand. Its design becomes variety. No different than the rose is the beauty and fragrance of a unified human family. The human family can only be unified when we allow each other respect. Respect for one another can only come when we learn to appreciate the mutual design of humanity.

Law Number One—Know and Respect Yourself

Law Number Two—Know and Respect Others

Law Number Three—Respect the Laws of Nature

Law Number Four—Appreciate the Mutual Design of Humanity

13

Appreciate the Accomplishments and the Intelligence of Others

Rule #5 in the *Commandments of Peace*

"Two thousand, one hundred, thirty-one, Cal Ripken, Jr. Stands Alone" was the caption on the special collector's edition of *Sports Illustrated*. After starting 2,130 games, playing 19,222 innings, appearing 9,327 times at the plate and batting more than 8,303 times, it was his night. This was his night to make history. Over the span of 14 years Ripken had earned the title of baseball's greatest "Iron Man." For twenty-two minutes on the night of September 6, 1995, the ball game between the California Angels and Baltimore Orioles came to a stop. As orange and black balloons were launched high into the skies above Oriole Park at Camden Yards, Whitney Houston sang, "One Moment in Time." The music was dampened by the thunder of applause and shouts cheering on and inaugurating the new king of the most consecutive games ever played in baseball.

The crowd cheered; some wept. Two thousand one hundred thirty one was the magic number that broke the record number of consecutive games played by Lou Gehrig. This is not the only record surpassed by Ripken. As of this writing, he also holds records for:

- Most consecutive games played at one position;
- Most consecutive games played at shortstop;
- Most consecutive innings played;
- Most consecutive errorless games played;
- Most assists in a season;
- Most All-Star Games as a shortstop;
- Most consecutive years as an All-Star Game starter;
- Most years leading the league in double plays;
- Rookie of the Year and MVP honors in back to back years; and
- Only player on a sub-.500 team to be voted MVP.

In addition, Ripken set other records. We can safely conclude he is well positioned to be accepted into the Baseball Hall of Fame. With all his records, his big record surpassing Lou Gehrig, was not a world's record. The world record was held by a Japanese player named Sachio Kinugasa. From September 6, 1995, the "Iron Man" would have to play consecutively 84 more games to tie, and 85 games to surpass the world record of 2,215. One June 14, 1996, he did!

Why did we care so little? Was this, too, not a great accomplishment by this superman of sports? Why was there no media hype? Was it that American spirit of bigotry and prejudice hovering once again over the American scene that blinded us of the accomplishments of others?

Appreciating other bodies of iron?

There is a lady. She has worked for the past twenty years. She has been watching children, allowing their parents to work, earning a living to provide for the health, safety, and growth of a child who theoretically may be a future president of our nation. She gets no media attention.

There is a man who works in a hospital. He hasn't had a vacation in ten years. He changes the bedding and cleans the rooms, including the floors and toilets. Sometimes the sheets are soiled with blood, feces, urine, and vomit. He gets no media attention.

There is a man who scales electric poles after storms, restoring light and power to many. There are reporters, mail carriers, plumbers, doctors, teachers, ministers, sanitation workers, store clerks, and service attendants of all types. All represent types of people who have gone to work diligently, year after year, never missing a day. These are the real "Iron Men and Women" who keep our nation and world in motion. Sick or well, many are committed to diligence. Some are too poor to even take the time to rest. Some men and women are working two, three, four, or more jobs per week. To lie down, for some, must wait for a casket. How much do we appreciate these people?

We are awestruck by Ripken. We fail to remember his time off during the off-seasons. We forget the fun once shared in a kid's game and how many of us, if not but once in a flash of a second, dreamed of suiting up in the uniform of our favorite team. Some of us forget about the opportunities for travel, the training camps in Florida and the dollars paid for one year of service. We also forget about the long strike that brought an end to the 1994 season. When the players decided to strike, vendors were hurt. Their strike brought a halt to the barkers, some college students who ran up and down the stadium stands selling beer, popcorn, Cokes, pretzels, and the all-American hot dog. We forgot about the lonely people and senior citizens who were happy to turn on the radio or television tuning into games as they sat in isolation. Some of these have worked many years, never losing a day. How much do we appreciate them? Ripken did a great job. I salute him and his family, including Mr. Ripken, Sr. and Mrs. Ripken, his mother. His mother did not share much of the limelight but we all know she raised one fine son. But, why the celebration? Why the preoccupation?

Every day should be a day of celebration. Each day should be a celebration of life. We should celebrate by appreciating the many wonderful people worldwide who make our lives a bit easier. The one who milks the cow, the one who grows the grain, picks the oranges, gathers the eggs, churns the butter, jellies the fruits, and collects the coffee beans is responsible for the items stocking our stores. Processors, labelers, packers, fuelers, transporters, and checkers who rapidly move our staple resources from a raw state, to our exchange state, where the items are purchased for our consumption are also essential.

When you add the bed you sleep on, the toothpaste and mouthwash you use, the water you drink, the clothing you wear, or the floor on which you stand each day, you have made use of hundreds of people. God may have made it all possible, but through the human family, most goods at your disposal are gifts through the accomplishments and intelligence of others. This we should celebrate.

We know very little about the many people with whom we are in contact daily. A simple cotton shirt has the logical backing of many who moved it from seed to sale. The package itself required several persons.

Each day, in America, from the time we open our eyes to the time we leave our homes, we are supplied freely, or at cost by the technical support of many. They have no faces but behind each tangible object is a story. That story is our interdependence on each other. It is the story of others' contributions and ours. How can we not appreciate the accomplishments and intelligence of others?

Contributors to the Scene

In 1968, the Dodd, Mead & Company publishers, located in New York, released a book by Irmengarde Eberle entitled, *Famous Inventors for Young People*. This book was originally copyrighted in 1941 under the name, *Famous Inventors for Boys and Girls*. This book included fifteen inventors:

Johannes Gutenberg
James Watt
Edmund Cartwright
Robert Fulton
Eli Whitney
George Stephenson
Samuel F. B. Morse
Cyrus Hall McCormick

    Henry Bessermer
    Gottlieb Daimler
    Alexander Graham Bell
    Thomas Alva Edison
    Wilbur and Orville Wright
    Guglielmo Marconi

In 1968, I was beginning my formal schooling. I was in the first grade. My oldest brother, Carl, and oldest sister, Vena, were beginning their last year of high school. Reading *Famous Inventors for Young People* was significant and very indicative of the education received by Carl and Vena, and the education I was about to receive. Each of the biographies were of White males. Somehow, this coincides with my belief that my public and private education implicitly taught the evolution of humanity, both technical and social, was the result of men, and especially men of European descent.

Couple this with the view of Charles Murray and Richard Herrnstein, *(The Bell Curve)*, who claim the hereditary superiority of Caucasians and the inferior intellect of Blacks, and you have succeeded in producing a formula for prejudice, bias, chauvinism, bigotry, hatred, cynicism, jealousy, and all the other wrongs that destroy the fabric of humanity. There is no truth to any race's claim to superiority.

The nation and world in which we live has been molded and shaped by many peoples. Africans, native Americans, Asians, South Americans, Hispanics, Indians, Mideasterners, people of both genders have played a great role in the advancement of our world. The next time you use liquid paper, "white out," or any other like brand of correction fluids, remember it was a woman who invented it. Her name was Bette Nesmith Graham. She is the mother of guitarist Michael Nesmith, who played for the chart-topping Monkees during the 1960s. It may seem insignificant, but her saving of time in typing pools, offices, homes, and campuses, as students completed term papers and reports has placed this former high school dropout at the head of a multi-million dollar corporation.

The next time you hear of a life saved by a bullet-proof vest or fire proof clothing, think of Stephanie Louise Kwolek, the DuPont scientist who holds more than 28 different patents in her specialty, which is low-temperature polymerization. She is the inventor of Kevlar. Kevlar is a synthetic fiber, light weight, and in many ways stronger than steel. This material is also used in steel-belted radial tires.

The next time you see beautiful hair curled by a curling iron, think of America's first African-American female millionaire. The inventor of the curling iron and straightening comb, modernized and used by cosmetologists worldwide, was Sarah Breedlove. She was known to many by her trade name, Madam C.J. Walker, after her husband Charles Walker. This successful entrepreneur was not only an inventor, but a pioneer of civil justice. Mrs. Walker died on May 25, 1919. She left legacies to scores of charitable and educational organizations. In her obituary, W.E.B. DuBois eloquently wrote, "It is given to few persons to transform a people in a generation. Yet this was done by the late Madam C.J. Walker."

The next time you use a flare to signal people to use caution ahead or warn of emergencies, think of Martha Cotton who developed, manufactured, and marketed them. During the Civil War, Cotton Night Signals were vital communication devices. These devices were used by the United States Navy to signal messages and warnings at night. Much of the credit to her invention was stolen by the U.S. Navy, because she was a woman.

The preceding examples are of females who have contributed to everyday life in our world. But what about other people who have made major contributions? During the eighteenth century, transportation along the Chesapeake region of America was by canoes. Canoes were the invention of Native Americans who constructed the water-going transports by burning out the interior of large logs. Canoes were essential to the tobacco trade which made that region rich. Today, canoeing is recreational. The aluminum and fiberglass constructed boats paddled along rivers and streams are reminders of the creativity of Native Americans.

Stepping out of the canoe and moving across land may require the wearing of shoes. Shoes are worn the world all over. Very few people appreciate the fact that Jan Matzeliger, born 1852, was the inventor of the shoe lasting machine. Fewer knew that he was Black. Shoe lasting was assembling shoes by a sturdy cotton or worsted cloth by hand over a foot-shaped iron. Matzeliger's invention changed the entire industry and made the skill of shoe lasting by hand obsolete. The next time you stroll in your shoes through the mall, grocery, or office supply store, think of calculators, cash registers, word processors, and automation systems. Think of Wang. In 1951, Dr. An Wang, born February 7, 1920 in Shanghi China, began his company, Wang laboratories. Beginning with his savings of $600, he parlayed a company with sales greater than $2.5 billion and a payroll covering some 20,000 employees based on contracts and orders for office furniture.

On January 28, 1986, in the company of Christa McAuliffe, Greg Jarvis, Judy Resnick, Mike Smith, Dick Scobee, and Ron McNair, another oriental American, Lt. Col. Ellison Onizuka, left an imprint of heroism on the world scene. This crew representing six religions, three ethnic groups, seven home states, men and women, military and civilian, and seven areas of professional expertise, was the crew of the Challenger. Friends, family, and people the world over, seventy three seconds after lift off, witnessed an explosion that tragically ended the flight and lives of the crew.

Astronaut Ellison S. Onizuka could best be remembered by readers of this message delivered to the Konawaena High Schools class of 1980:

> If I can impress on you, only one idea tonight, let it be that the people who make this world run, whose lives can be termed successful, whose names will go down in the history books, are not the cynics, the critics, or the armchair quarterbacks. They are the adventurers, the explorers, and doers of this world. When they see a wrong or a problem, they do something about it. When they see a vacant place in our knowledge, they work to fill that void. Rather than leaning back and criticizing

how things are, they work to make things the way they should be. They are the aggressive, the self-starters, the innovative, and the imaginative of this world. Every generation has the obligation to free men's minds for a look at new worlds . . . to look out from a higher plateau than the last generation. Your vision is not limited by what your eye can see, but by what your mind can imagine. Many things that you take for granted were considered unrealistic dreams by previous generations. If you accept these past accomplishments as common place, then think of the new horizons that you can explore. From your vantage point, your education and imagination will carry you to places which you won't believe possible. Make your life count, and the world will be a better place because you tried.

Who can forget the mighty voice of the Rev. Dr. Martin Luther King, Jr., that shook America on August 28, 1963, when he related his dream in which the "sons of former slaves and sons of former slave owners will be able to sit down together at the table of brotherhood." A dream in which his "four little children will one day live in a nation where they will not be judged by the color of their skin, but by the content of their character." A dream that would "be able to transform the jangling discords of our nation into a beautiful symphony of brotherhood." By which "faith we will be able to work together, to pray together, to stand up for freedom together, knowing that we will be free one day."

Dr. King envisioned a day when "all of God's children will be able to sing with new meaning: 'My country 'tis if thee; sweet land of liberty of thee I sing; land where my father's died, land of the pilgrim's pride; from every mountain side, let freedom ring.' " In closing that momentous speech, summoning the conscience of a divided nation, he further stated,

> When we allow freedom to ring, when we let it ring
> from every village and hamlet, from every state and
> city, we will be able to speed up that day when all of
> God's children—Black men and White men, Jews and

Gentiles, Protestants and Catholics—will be able to join hands and sing in the words of the old Negro Spiritual, "Free at last, free at last; thank God Almighty, we are free at last."

Today our freedom as a people, as a nation, and a world is held in check. In the words of poet, Carl Sandburg, "Nothing happens unless first a dream." Sandburg's statement may be the echo of Solomon who wrote, "Where there is no vision the people perish" (Proverbs 29:18).

Open your eyes! Be bold! Dream! Envision a world appreciative and respectful of the accomplishments and the intelligence of others. You will find in your sights more harmony. In more harmony, you will find cooperation, in cooperation you will find opportunity. In opportunity to all, you will find hope. In hope, you will find comfort. In comfort, you will find peace.

Law Number One—Know and Respect Yourself

Law Number Two—Know and Respect Others

Law Number Three—Respect the Laws of Nature

Law Number Four—Appreciate the Mutual Design of Humanity

Law Number Five—Appreciate the Accomplishments and Intelligence of Others

14

Be Honest, Never Patronizing

Rule #6 in the *Commandments of Peace*

"This is Mr. Hunt. He will be playing the piano. Please escort him to the front," the usher was instructed before proceeding to the front of the church. In a voice loud enough to wake the dead, the usher instructed Mr. Hunt to follow her. She took his hand and led the talented musician to his seat. Mr. Hunt had a physical limitation. He had no eyesight. I am certain he saw the usher in his mind's eye and recognized her limitation. She could not differentiate between blindness and deafness.

"Gosh! You really look lovely today." She was told by her boss, "If I weren't married, you'd be mine tonight." I am certain the boss intended no harm. He was just making conversation. I am also certain, the rule governing sexual harassment would apply. Besides his balding head, short stature, pale complexion, and beer gut hiding his belt and obstructing his personal view of his feet, he may not have appealed to the woman.

"Let me tell you what the Catholics teach and believe," the minister loudly proclaimed. "The Pope is God! We all know that there is one God and besides Him there is no other." This untruth was spoken to men and women who might not realize this is false. Those with Catholic friends or relatives realized the minister was wrong; others believed his mistaken words.

"I tell you what the Jews are up to. It's all about money and power. They are atheists seeking to control the world." Passively, it is taught by Christians everywhere that no Jews practicing Judaism can enter heaven. It is a Christian belief from the teachings of the New Testament:

> Jesus instructed His followers to go everywhere and tell the Good News. Tell it to everyone. Relate that they have found the Christ. Relate the witness of His death and resurrection. To those who, by faith, believe their testimony and is baptized will be saved. (St. Mark 16: 15-16)

or "Because God so loved the world He ransomed His only son. So that anyone who believes in His son will not truly die but enjoy life eternally" (St. John 3:16).

No Christian can hate Jews. Jews are a tremendously blessed group of Hebrew descendants making it into God's kingdom. St. Paul wrote in the eleventh chapter of his letter to the Romans: ". . . all Israel shall be saved as it is written."

The eleventh chapter tells how, in Isaiah 40, the Supremacy of God is implied by reason. St. Paul asks:

1. Who has measured the oceans in the palm of his hand?
2. Who has used his hand to measure the sky?
3. Who has used scales to weigh the mountains and hills?
4. Who has known the mind of the Lord?
5. Who has been able to give the Lord advice?
6. Whom did the Lord ask for help?
7. Who taught Him the right way?
8. Who taught the Lord knowledge?
9. Who showed Him the way to understanding?
10. Who created the stars?

St. Paul asks, "Can you compare God to anything . . . or anyone?" St., Paul wonders, "who can know the mind of the Lord?"

Shades of Gray

We all possess positive and negative qualities. We were made in the image and likeness of an Almighty and Supreme Being. In Him and through Him we find our perfected selves. When we are good, we resemble God.

In crisis, we tend to perform altruistically as angels. We rush to disaster, giving sympathy and aid to those in distress. We empty our hearts in prayer and hope. We empty our pockets giving help. As mean-spirited as we may seem, the majority of us have hearts tender enough to care. This shade of gray is positive. This shade of gray is the colorful content of light. This light of humanity, backed by a cosmic and infinite force, is the flame blazing high on the torch of hope. I appeal to the finest in men and women.

From day to day, many of us are overcome by weakness. No crisis is at hand. We are mere sharers of space, residents and occupants of earth. We share a common history of self-ishness. It promotes the "survival of the fittest" instinct in us. Selfishness puts us at odds critically judging intents. It is the birthplace of resentment and hatred. It is our willingness to strangle the beauty from life. We are blinded more than Mr. Hunt, to the light that lifts us. We are shielded from the radiance that defines our commonality as brothers and sisters. We are deafened, more than the insensitive and offensive boss, from the sounds that unite us by laughter, tear, speech, and song.

Here the shade of gray is darkened. All the color of life is absorbed and gloom prevails. As snakes, we hiss at each other, viperously, darting poison into the neck of humanity. Rodney King asked on the night of the verdict which found his evil assailants not guilty, "Can't we all just get along?"

I will die with the hope and dream blazing in my mind, that we can! God granted us all free will. We choose good. We choose evil. We make the choices as our feet march to the beats of light and darkness. We make the choices that lift or defeat the human family. We make up the world. It is our choice how to live. It is our God given free will.

We Stand Where We Choose

It was Aristotle, the Greek philosopher, who lived between 384 and 322 B.C., who wrote, "Some men are just as sure of the truth of their opinions as are others of what they know." We stand where we choose.

Joseph Joubert, in Pensées wrote, "Those who never retract their opinions, love themselves more than they love truth." We stand where we choose.

William Blake, in *The Marriage of Heaven and Hell* wrote: "The man who never alters his opinion is like standing in water, and breeds reptiles of the mind." We stand where we choose.

Elizabeth Drew, in *The Modern Novel*, wrote, "The world is not run by thought, nor by imagination, but by opinion." We stand where we choose.

Alfred Austin in *Prince Lucifer*, wrote "Public opinion is no more than this: what people think, that other people think." We stand where we choose.

If asked, where do we stand on many of the issues confronting us today, many would respond based on unthinking, unreasoned agreement with public opinion. In America, we are guided by popular and public opinion. This is not bad when the public opinion is positive and in harmony with natural law which yields natural rights to the human family. However, when public opinion is bad, oppressive, and invasive upon our natural liberties and we passively follow, the heart and soul of the human family are wounded.

Consider Ireland. Catholics and Protestants continue to use the sword. Death and destruction lurk over minds swallowed into a swamp of darkness. Nobody wants to die. Nobody wants destruction. As adults assault each other in their quest for power, the fallout is seen as a fading hope in the eyes of their children. The adults stand where they choose. It is sad that war is chosen over children.

War is a choice throughout our world. In the crossfire are children, innocent babies, born by fate, not by choice, into the hotbeds of hate. How can we be a moral people and not stand for peace?

The major battles fought today stem from the lack of respect for differing views. Groups of oppressed people are taunted into resentment. They react with violence, trying to free themselves from misguided opinions which result in discrimination. They fight to free themselves of systematized persecution.

This model is clear in America. Recently, politicians and political organization have attacked the weak in our society. Bashing minorities and the poor has become a blood sport. Lies have colored public opinion. The result is disunion and resentment. Today the most powerful sword known in America is the dollar. The fallout from its wrongful use hurts children most.

Cheating is the skill that advances the game. We cry out against tax and spend only to replace it with borrow and spend. The fallout is hurting the children upon whose backs are placed the nation's debts for generations to come.

We beg the nation to limit programs designed to prevent crime and in its place beg for more spending to erect more prisons. Neglected children, later take up penal residence in these prisons.

We bash the gays, the poor, women, the handicapped, and we campaign hypocritically against immigrants. Glamour and glory are wooing us to vain and selfish pursuits. Our children are damaged, ruining our posterity. Our opinions are our reflections blazing out from the mirror of truth. We stand where we choose.

When we learn of the unruliness and lawlessness of the nation's young, when we push hope for our future only to be pushed back by apathy, remember this. The children in whom we invest our hope, are the same ones we taught. If they hate, we taught them; if they love, we showed them. If they are ignorant, we allowed it. If they are free thinkers and respectful, we trusted them. Our nation's children, our world's children, good or bad, are the images released from the mirror bearing our reflections. We are who we choose to be.

Our Tomorrow's, Our Hope

Look into the mirror of history. Be honest. What can we see? Let's use Columbus Day. In the U.S., the second Monday of October is observed as a legal holiday. This day was set aside to honor Christopher Columbus, as we were taught. The Spanish explorer's discovery of America: "In fourteen hundred and ninety two, Columbus sailed the ocean blue." Every land has its legends. America is no different. Columbus never made it to America. Considering he set out to find a new route to India by going west, he was a failure. Columbus Day is really a day set aside as a memorial to the settlement of Europeans on the continent now known as America. It draws attention to the oppression and usurpation of the Native Americans. It goes back to the hubris that gave rise to slavery. It is the cause of a war, in which brother would struggle against brother. It is what denied women participation in democracy. This cavalier attitude remains part of the American scene today.

Some people recognize the lies of the traditional history books. Some realize that important contributions have come from men and women of all races from throughout the world.

When we clean the mirror of our past and see our ways of teaching and learning honestly reflected, we will bring as a gift to our tomorrow's hope. Collectively, we are the "Image of Our Individuality."

One day, my manager invited me on an outside walk around my office. He looked at me and said, "Don, I don't have a problem with Black people." He further explained, as if I asked of his Norwegian background. He related how people made fun of him because of his Norwegian stature. I cared, but if he was trying to relate his experience with a people forced into slavery, subjected to hundreds of years of subhuman treatment, denied a legal right to read and write, under constant attack and watch of hatemongers, such as the Ku Klux Klan and the White Resistance Movement, if he was trying to equate himself, being made fun of, with men and women set upon by dogs, washed along the sidewalks with fire hoses, stoned, burned, and hanged, as they sought out civil rights, civil justice, and civil respect, he was very wrong.

Hatred and discontent streamed from his heart. He offered, "What would you say if I told you I would allow my daughter to date a Black guy?" I wondered silently what special quality his daughter had that would make her worthy to share the company of an ebony-rich man of African descent? I said nothing in reply.

Since the 1980 election of Ronald Reagan, a number of doors have swung open. These open doors have revealed the oppressors of our society. Doors concealing hatred against women, minorities, immigrants, socio-economic structures, and religious thoughts once protected, opened to the public arena. The so-called moral majority led the charge.

Today, eruptions of intolerance spew magma of hate everywhere. Leaders of our nation are at the front of the pack, promoting disunion by their rhetoric. Young bigots are formed, fashioned by the patterns of bigots. Jesse Jackson, Joseph Lowery, Hosea Williams, and others are demonized as Jesse Helms, Strom Thurmon, and other antagonists of civil justice are praised. Franklin Roosevelt said in 1936, "A government can be no better than the public opinion which sustains it." If America is to change, its citizenry must change. As individuals, we must promote tolerance and respect for all people.

A Ray of Light Beyond the Clouds

I must confess, Ralph Reed and William Bennett found no place in my heart. Their often misinformed and reckless shelling of those traditionally disrespected by the "in crowds" of America is indefensible. Reed, a hero of the Christian Right, a political puppet of the Republican machine, displayed himself as highly opinionated and carelessly disrespectful of many people whose ancestry helped to build and sustain this nation.

William Bennett displayed himself as a Republican instrument whose only claim to national fame was his tenure at the Department of Education. He produced a report to tell America its schools were in trouble.

One Sunday, I was watching "Meet the Press" or "Face the Nation." Two of the guests were Bennett and Reed. I listened as they discussed recent church burnings. Joseph Lowery, President of the Southern Christian Leadership Conference, had charged that because of people like Reed and his followers, antagonists of civil rights, the backdrop had been set for church burnings.

With anger Reed began to respond. Soon, as if guided by the hand of God, he began to digress. He quickly admitted that the Christian Right has been on the wrong side of the struggle for civil rights. He was soon echoed by Bill Bennettt. Are my prayers that these men of high profile and ability to persuade, slowly being answered? I don't know. I do, however, believe the Lord's spirit that spoke to Samuel, the 11th Century Hebrew judge and first of the great prophets, saying, "People look at the outside of a person but God looks at the heart." Perhaps they can evict the demons of hatred, the beast of bigotry, the fiends of prejudice. Maybe through their leadership, that Satanic force of intolerance can be subdued and the glory of a loving and inclusive God revealed. From beyond the clouds of darkness, darts a ray of hope.

Another ray of hope I found in a magazine, the *Christian Century:* "SBC Renounces Racist Past." On June 20, 1995, the Southern Baptist Convention voted to adopt a resolution renouncing its racist roots. It further apologized for its past defense of slavery. Nearly 20,000 members were in attendance at the SBC's 150th anniversary held at Atlanta's Georgia Dome. The SBC delegates were challenged to "unwaveringly denounce racism, in all of its forms as a deplorable sin," and "lament and repudiate historical acts of evil as slavery from which we continue to reap a bitter harvest." An apology, on behalf of the 15.6 million member denomination, to all African-Americans was offered for "condoning and/or perpetuating individual and systematic racism in our lifetime." The resolution also offered repentance for "racism . . . [of which they] have been guilty whether consciously or unconsciously." They pledged to eradicate racism in all forms from Southern Baptist life and ministry.

The racism resolution marked the first time the predominantly White denomination dealt specifically with the issue of slavery. It was the first formal acknowledgment that racism played a role in its founding. In more recent history, Southern Baptists have, "failed in many cases to support and in some cases, opposed legitimate initiatives to secure the civil rights of African-Americans." Many of the affiliate congregations have, "intentionally and/or unintentionally excluded Blacks from worship." Holding the torch for which this book is written, Gary Frost, the second vice-president of the SBC, stated "Our nation is being ripped apart by hatred." He noted that, "It is up to the church of Jesus Christ to begin the process of true reconciliation." How powerful! Which U.S. President will be willing to follow that lead? Perhaps one not swayed by politics, political correctness, and contributions can muster the fortitude.

Stand Up!

Celebrating Black History month is good but it will not serve to link and educate Americans about the achievements, pride and promise that built our nation. Honoring the birthday of the slain civil rights leader and evangelist of peace for all people, the Reverend Dr. Martin Luther King, Jr., will not serve to bridge the socio-political breach that divides us. These celebrations are great and should continue to be promoted. Such celebrations serve to remind Americans of the genius buried deep in American history. These celebrations promote brotherhood and solidarity.

But never should the day in January or the days in February be seen as a cure for race relations. Never should race relations be viewed as a cure all for social ills. When this occurs, we unfold our well-taught American ability to patronize. Patronization occurs when we adopt an air of condescension toward others on the basis of physical, mental, economic, or even spiritual make-up. Condescension occurs when we patronize others. Patronizing is the end result when we falsely give attention to our differences and artificially lift members of our society on insincere platforms.

Many Americans know of Dr. King and his efforts, promoting civil equality and respect. Very few know of the stories behind the faces who made the struggle for civil rights a necessity. Far fewer will understand the needs of women, gays, immigrants, the disabled and the poor for civil justice and equality.

Take time. Come close. Listen. Hear the heartbeat of America. Come closer, hear the pulsation of our world. Hear in a distance, the rhythm of peace. Step by step, it is marching. Every beat of a drum sounded by the drum majors of peace is moving closer. Hear the far off sounds of trumpets, blasting the call for unity. Are you in step? Look around. Are those with whom you share company moving to join the freedom march? Are you ready to join in the chorus raising your voice for peace?

Stand up! Stand up for peace! Stand up for justice! Stand up for unity! Stand up for righteousness! Stand up for the children! Stand up for respect! Stand up for our future! And when you have done all you could, when you have cared, when you have held high that blazing torch for peace, when you feel you can do no more, stand. Help will come. Stand!

Take Time to Notice

Think! Most of our knowledge of others is based on second-hand information formed on opinion and speculation. Our first hand intimate knowledge of people who differ from us is extremely limited. Be honest, never patronizing, is my advice. Take time to say hello to a neighbor or even a stranger who may differ from you. Throw out your concepts of them. Come to learn of individuals and the things we have in common. Come to know those close by. Look honestly for the things which are positive. A whole new world will unfold.

Law Number One—Know and Respect Yourself

Law Number Two—Know and Respect Others

Law Number Three—Respect the Laws of Nature

Law Number Four—Appreciate the Mutual Design of Humanity

Law Number Five—Appreciate the Accomplishments
and Intelligence of Others

Law Number Six—Be Honest, Never Patronizing

15

Avoid Blanket Statements

Rule #7 in the *Commandments of Peace*

In the English language, a noun defines a person, a place, or thing. Many times, when we describe a noun in the aggregate, denoting a grouping of a common type, a collective noun is used. A collective noun is a noun in singular form that denotes a group. For example, one may speak of the following: a family, a band, a public, or a committee. Each of the words is a singular form of a noun. Each noun describes a body of individuals bound together by a common relationship.

The English language has an abundance of collective nouns describing groups of things, especially animals. Here is a sample of terms referring to groups:

a bale of turtles
a bed of clams
a brood of chicks
a cast of hawks
a cloud of gnats
a colony of ants
a crash of rhinoceri
a down of hares
a drove of cattle
a flight of birds
a flock of sheep

a gaggle of geese
a grist of bees
a herd of elephants
a kindle of kittens

If a mob (of kangaroos), should suddenly swarm (like bees), over a tribe (of goats), and a flock (of birds), a pair (of horses), a school (of fish), don't worry. There's always a sleuth (of bears), keeping watch (like nightingales), over the nest (of vipers).

Moving Ahead

As we reach into the twenty first century, we are reaching into an era which aligns with the original intentions of our Creator. It is Biblically and naturally implied we were and are created as free moral agents. I understand this since we are free to choose our behavior. Although we share many similarities in our human groupings, such as skin color, eye color, body type, natural color and texture of hair, and sexual design, we differ from animals by our intelligence and individuality. Even as conformists, as I will explain, we are people of free will. In America, although not exclusively, this right is guarded and defended, as long as it does not encroach upon the same freedoms of others. This free will was established in the U.S. Constitution.

Our Individuality

As humans, we are individuals. Our characters are defined by our physical, mental, and social composition. First, as individuals, we carry the physical and distinct stampings of our hereditary. We are marked by our regional origins and family. I bear a striking resemblance to my father. My brothers do as well. No doubt we are sons of Francis Emory Harris. My father, in many ways, duplicates the physical image of his father. No doubt he is Granddad Emory's son. With our ebony skin, large lips, and wide noses, we all proudly display the stampings of our race. Standing together, we differ physically by size, audibly by voice, and genealogically by age.

Secondly, as individuals, we carry the mental stampings of our inborn abilities and experience. Depending on our birth, nutritional development, and life experiences, we are mentally molded and shaped. Our mental abilities, in conjunction with our exposure to life and the many combinations offered, cause us to act in the ways we do. Thus, we are individuals by character.

Our characters are established from the moment of conception. At conception, DNA is copied into the cells and multiplied. This process develops positive and negative traits. By our intrinsic and personal experiences of daily life, our traits will develop into strengths and weaknesses. It is on this level of mental development that we intellectually, whether positive or negative, trade with society. Here we share as much of ourselves as we choose. Here we accept the teachings of others. Here is decided how much of each, in this giving and taking, we are willing to trade out, or mirror the environments of which we live. To conform or not to conform with society is our decision, as to how much of an individual we are willing to be.

Our ability to conform is positive and good for the safety and survival of humanity. To aid our societies, laws have been established. Obedience of the law protects us from chaos. The more technologically advanced we become, the more we need and rely upon law for protection. This is best described by the use of traffic signals. Non-conformity or disobedience can set the stage for catastrophe. On the other hand, conformity can be negative, as in the case of hatred embraced by one group of people, which when acted on suppresses, or oppresses another. This is best described by hate groups whose members conform to the model of ignorance. This is ineffective in that it causes others to react, thus conforming to the call of leaders responding to hatred. It is good when individuals are positively prompted to practice peace. It can be vile when people venomously choose violence to vitiate the oppressor. Not only do we carry the mental stampings of our personal experience, but we must identify with the collective experiences of our heritage. Here, as individuals, we choose how much our individuality will display with the large or small world in which we live.

As individuals, we are social animals. Some of us pattern schools of fish: they travel in lock-step formation fearing falling from the social family of which they have chosen. Others pattern well-trained domesticated types. They have more independence and present themselves as distinct character types.

Some members of our human family, known as society, will trade off almost the entirety of themselves to mirror what they feel are the expectation and measure of a truly civilized and just human. They tend to be the faddish. Their taste is aligned with, and in harmony with, the latest. They are in step with the trends of food, fashion, and a facsimile of political and religious thought. Many times, depending on their depth of conformity, they are disturbed by the few intruders swimming against the direction traveled by their school of fish. Many of them are soon after the encounter returned to united formation to continue their travel. Only rarely are some swallowed by the big fish of social disaster.

Other members of our society are not as willing to trade off themselves. They are strong. They are bold and brave, hold tight-fisted to their individuality. They are the sellers known as the movers and shakers. They trade off very little of themselves or mirror the conforming masses. Oddly, they are liberal, as well as conservative. They are willing to fight for the future of the human family and the planet on which we live.

Some of these individuals are stuck in the muddy past. Others are presented with eyes bulging with excitement in anticipation of the newness only known by tomorrow. Constantly, they are in conflict. Together, they build up and tear down our world. Together, they invent and develop new challenges, as they grapple over the center represented by conformists. This fixed inclination, to the ongoing construction and destruction of our world, is in constant alignment with natural law. By this process, the world is constantly refined, refreshed, replenished, recreated, reinvigorated, and renewed as it continues to evolve.

The builders and destroyers who construct and deconstruct our world, are constantly demanding the attention of political and religious social agendas. They press upon those fearful of asserting their own individuality and promote differences, indifference, and exclusion. On this level, it works for the good and evil of humanity. No blanket statement can truly, or adequately represent the people. We are different from all other animals. We are people represented, as free moral agents. We are individual people of choice.

Breaking It Down

Much of our chosen behavior is prompted by our comfort levels within our natural and social environments. On the natural side, in the technologically advanced society, we don't hate the heat of summer. We are stressed. Due to the introduction of artificial coolness by air conditioning, our bodies have fallen out of sync with nature. Many of us find it hard to contend with the natural patterns of the seasons.

On the social side; we do not truly hate tall men with polka-dotted skin and green hair. But to not risk the ridicule for being out of step with accepted popular opinion, we find it politically correct to do so. If accepted popular society dictates, we will climb any mountain and ford any stream to follow any trend. As in the example of Jews, who were destroyed by an evil Nazi-led Germany, some were willing to subvert the right, as they dashed for the wrong, hoping to stay in step with popular beliefs. This is the view held deep in the secret of successful advertisers and promoters of goods and services. Their message is, keep in step.

In a positive sense, this view affirms our distinct cultures. It also unites us, as groups of people, as our individual or collective bodies, contribute to the quilt of humanity. In a negative sense, the quilt is destroyed. Thread by thread, the human quilt is unraveled. New threads of plainness are introduced, lacking individualism in design. It carries on the process of dismantling natural beauty. We must always be on a constant mission, building a better and more positive society. A positive society is rich. It respects fairness to all. It draws out and appreciates the individual. It restores beauty to the quilt, representing the human family. If your conforming places undue burdens and stresses on others, back off. Chances are you are out of step with the laws of peace.

We must also be on a faithfully constant mission of deconstruction. We must destroy the things that separate us as a human family. The things that separate us are the things that limit respect, causing us to look down on others. This is accomplished by the outward signs of humanity, race, gender, age, economics, education, political and religious affiliation. Individuals are not stereotypes and the real person is the individual. These are the things that limit fairness, favoring some with a head start of opportunity.

To Bring It Home

A good example is the frivolous use of the word "they." Based on nature, as in the case of language, the pronoun "they" is usually used to identify groups of people bound by a common characteristic. "They," in all its forms such as, "those people" are generalizing and pigeonholing terms. "They" creates many of the problems confronting our world. It creates an obstacle to peace.

Here are some forms of "they" and "those people" that, when followed by unfounded opinion, serve only to irritate, aggravate, and infuriate, provoking hostilities, thus dividing us in every way:

They act	They do	They lack
They are	They don't	They need
They believe	They feel	They see
They can	They have	They want
They can't	They haven't	They will
They won't		

"They," like "these people," when used irresponsibly, blankets groups of people of which we have limited knowledge. Perhaps this explains our fascination with people representing groups originally frowned upon, who surprisingly rise to prominence.

Disrespectful blanket statements are made in a number of generalizing ways. However done, it only serves to increase hostility and distrust. It indicts humanity with ignorance. It breaks down communication and tears asunder the bands that bind us as a human family. It becomes a poison to peace.

Replace "they" or "those people" with any other nouns such as:

Rich people	Handicapped people	Single people
Poor people	Oriental people	Old people
Men	Boys	Black men
Women	Girls	White men
Hispanics	Jews	Senior citizens

Catholic or Protestant, you have set the stage for a breakdown in social harmony. This is due to the heavy reliance on stereotyping.

This is most common with many minority groups under constant, although many times unintentional, oppression by a majority group. Identify a group and describe the bad aspects of it you've come to believe and expect. There is an old saying: "If you've got nothing good to say about someone it's best to keep your mouth shut."

Here's a better way. If you must speak of "they" or "those people," speak of the positives. Speak of their contributions to the betterment of our world. You will find growth in your circle of friends. We need to clean our minds of the poisons we've unknowingly ingested. Only then can we give peace a chance. Avoid speaking, writing, communicating about "them" in a negative sense. Besides, how can you describe all or the majority of any group if you have not met them all or live as they do?

The seventh law of peace calls for wisdom. This law in principle challenges us to avoid blanket statements. Avoid making blanket statements. We, as individuals, respect individuality. Become one again. A whole new world of beauty will unfold.

Law Number One—Know and Respect Yourself

Law Number Two—Know and Respect Others

Law Number Three—Respect the Laws of Nature

Law Number Four—Appreciate the Mutual Design of
                Humanity

Law Number Five—Appreciate the Accomplishments
                and Intelligence of Others

Law Number Six—Be honest, Never Patronizing

Law Number Seven—Avoid Blanket Statements

16

Respect the Right to Dissent

Rule #8 in the *Commandments of Peace*

What is dissent? Simply stated, to dissent is to differ from the opinion held by the majority. To be a dissenter is to freely exercise one's right not to conform. This is the practice of individuality at its highest level. If a panel of judges were to agree upon a decision with a judge or judges in the minority not willing to concur, we may logically conclude the minority holds a dissenting opinion or opinions. The right to dissent is another one of the many natural freedoms. Exerting this right has historically resulted in many wonderful things.

Dissenters to Name a Few

He was an Italian, Christoforo Colombo, known by the Spanish as Christobal Colon, known to Americans as Christopher Columbus, the explorer. He was born in 1451 at Genoa, Italy. At an early age, he settled in Lisbon, Portugal. Use of his sailing experience, reading from the second century A.D. Alexandrine scientist, Ptolemy, and second book of Esdras caused Columbus to conclude the earth was spherical. His view was dissent from the popular-and well-taught idea which described the earth as flat. His dissent gave birth to a new era. The era following his voyage of 1492 was the dawning of immigrants, who sailed rough seas, seeking a new world. Immigrants settled in America, increasing the population.

America was a nation where people were ruled by representative democracy, not royal fiat or decree.

He was Frederick Bailey, born into slavery in 1817 near Tuckahoe, Maryland. After his escape to freedom 21 years later, he changed his name to Frederick Augustus Douglas. He, too, was a dissenter. He was viewed as a bad slave and was sent to a slave breaker who worked and whipped him mercilessly. He endured this mistreatment until one day he could no longer stand it and fought back. He was a man whose natural rights were found in natural law. Natural law allowed dissent. His dissent set a fire deep in the spirits of abolitionists whose constant fight against moral inequities won the freedom of people living and yet to be born.

It was 1955. America had reached a turning point in civil relations. Little did America know, it was only opening a door which would challenge the conscious of its will, manifested in disrespect, to a people based on color alone. Little did they know, that very paper which declared their freedom and separation from an aggressively oppressive and disrespectful state would be challenged by its own words, "We hold theses truths to be self-evident that all men are created equal." The latter part of the 1950s brought a boom in Christian education, as many American Whites established private schools, as smoke screens to continue segregated systems of education. Few were naive and truly pushed for quality instruction, backed by positive Christian ethics and values in the teaching of their children. However, a direct correlation was demonstrated in the numbers gathered by the National Center for Education Statistics' Digest of Education Statistic and the U.S. Department of Education's Office of Educational Research and Improvement. In 1950, one religiously-affiliated school system boasted an enrollment of 3,066,387. After the 1954 Supreme Court ruling on Brown vs. Board of Education, which designated separate but equal schools for children unlawful, the number of children in church-affiliated schools rose steadily, peaking in 1960 at 5,253,791.

While many were amazed by the surprising level of fairness in the Supreme Court and optimistic that things were working for the better, they soon realized the heart of America was still stained with evil. Its beat was out of step by an arrhythmia of hatred. Even though laws were changed, America suffered with a congenital heart defect slowing the flow of peace.

On December 1, 1955, another dissenter rose to prominence. Her name was Rosa Parks. Her feet were tired after a long day's work. She boarded a bus for home. She was not out to begin a movement. But when she was led to move to the rear of that bus to make a seat available to a White man she found she was even more tired of the willful disrespect and social injustice that gave rise to such unjust regulations.

Other African-Americans conformed to the Jim Crow laws that denied natural laws of dignity. Such laws were ethnically discriminating by their legal enforcement and traditional sanctions. Surprisingly, such ignorance was widely practiced in the American bible belt. It is here that Mrs. Parks' dissent launched a movement. This movement called on the leadership of a new minister in town, Dr. Martin Luther King, Jr.

Dr. King, himself a dissenter, was called out of formation and, by nature's law, drafted to serve as a drum major. Mrs. Parks and a host of other dissenters organized a boycott. This boycott was the Montgomery Bus Boycott. For 381 days, Blacks picketed White businesses and refused to use public transportation. Their measures resulted in a 1956 ruling by the Supreme Court declaring Alabama's bus segregation laws unconstitutional. During the interim, more than Mrs. Parks had been arrested. King, too, was arrested, charged with staging an "illegal boycott."

The Power of One

It is the story of a man named David, known affectionately as little David. He was still in his youth when he decided to take on Goliath. The so-called "real men" were afraid to take on this man, described as a giant. Those who did take him on proved the fears to be well-founded.

Goliath stood, by Biblical accounting, 9 feet 9 inches tall. He terrified all who saw him. Goliath was proud of his fearfulness. This interested David who was weary of this display.

David considered his work as a shepherd. He thought of how well he tended his sheep. He remembered how when a bear took one of his sheep he smote the bear and made it release the sheep. He thought of the lion that he bravely grabbed by the mane, when the lion thought it safe to steal a sheep. He thought of his God. Many times he was made brave when he considered the Lord was his shepherd. Even if he walked in a valley, shadowed by evil, he could be brave, knowing the presence of a real, living, and concerned God was with him.

David decided to take Goliath on. Knowing this, the commander of the forces, challenged by this monster of a man and his people, suited him for battle. A brass helmet was put on his head. He was jacketed with plated armor and given a sword. These artifacts were too weighty and incommodious. David refused them. He went after Goliath with a simple sling-and-stone combination.

Backed God's providence, the shepherd boy, David, was face to face with the nemesis of his people. This amused Goliath. How ridiculous to send this boy after the Giant of Giants? Who would send a boy to do a man's job? As Goliath considered David's stature, David considered Goliath. As David's arm spun the stone, preparing it for flight, he focused on Goliath's massive head. Negative thinking would suggest he may miss but, "With a head that big, how could he miss," David thought.

"Goliath!" he said, "you come to me with a sword, spear and shield. I come to you, in the name of the Lord that you defied. Goliath!" he called charging with the stone winding up for launching. "Today that same Lord will deliver you into my hands. I will kill you. Afterward, I will remove your head and give your body to your people, to be eaten by the wild birds and beasts."

At this point, proving his trust in God, David ran faster, closer, releasing the stone. This stone guided by David's insight, faith in an Almighty and Protective God, sunk deep into his target, that big head of Goliath. Right between the eyes.

One man! One stone! One God! The popular opinion was to dress for war, run for cover. David chose to dissent. David was a positive thinker. Win or lose was his choice. He chose to win and with persistence he did. When Goliath fell, his eyes beheld the proof. It is not the size of a man that counts, or his willingness to conform, but his faith in God and self that annihilates any obstacle to peace. Backed by an infinite power, here is found the power of one.

Are you follower? Have you signed on to the latest form of political correctness? Have you consciously thought out what you can do that will help to bring about a social order of peace? Building more prisons will not solve our national problems. Putting more convicts to death will not stop murder. Limiting concern for the least in our world may save a dollar here and a few pennies there, but it will not lift the morale of the forgotten.

Selfish, inconsiderate, boastful, insidious men promote a strange nationalism that divides our nation and world. They insensitively broaden the gap between rich and poor. They obstruct justice. They blame the defenseless in our society for our national woes. They distort history in favor of one group. They parade themselves as patriotic as they damn the nation. They are many of our political leaders backed by conforming masses who have feasted from their tables of poison. In unison, they sneer and jeer at the intelligent dissenter whose eyes are open and disgusted with the status quo. These are the "ones out of sync." These are the ones, when allowing the reign of natural law, who seek and promote true peace. These are they who respect the laws of love, of which the greatest is, "love thy neighbor as thy self."

Love never demands agreement. Love calls for respect. The heart of love beats by compassion. The bounds of love are broad. The promise of love is salvation. Love allows trust. Love allows dissent.

What is Love?

Love defined, in the sense we need to make our point is defined as an energetically and enthusiastically warm attachment to others arising out of a natural kinship. It is displayed by an unselfish loyal and benevolent concern for the good of others.

This past weekend, I tuned into the services from the Crystal Cathedral at Garden Grove, California. Robert Anthony Schuller was delivering the sermon. He gave an illustration of love that I hope never to forget.

It was the story of Billy. Five minutes before the recess bell, Billy was found in a crisis. He had to get to the bathroom. He twisted and danced in his seat as he focused on the clock, waiting to be released from the class. "Five minutes," he counted hoping that time would pass quickly. "Four minutes, fifty seconds," he counted as he again reviewed the clock. "Four minutes, forty five seconds," in anticipation.

The teacher called on Billy to answer a question. Startled, Billy lost control. Into this seat, down his leg traveled the warm flow. It concluded, forming a puddle at his feet.

Billy sat in silence as the teacher went on to the next student. "How awful," he thought. "What will I do?" The kids will laugh at me, tease, and embarrass me. Billy began to pray. "Dear God help me! Don't let them see me like this."

After his prayer came Sarah. She was walking to the back of the class carrying a bowl of gold fish. Just a few steps from Billy, she stumbled losing balance, losing control of the bowl, fish, and water. The water splashed Billy, creating an even larger puddle on the floor. His pants were even wetter.

Billy won the sympathy of his classmates as he leaped from his seat asking, "How could you?" Off he went to put on his gym shorts. The students, in sympathy with Billy, cleaned up the watery mess as they ridiculed Sarah for her clumsiness.

All through recess, Billy witnessed Sarah's isolation and scorn from his classmates. Sarah's day was in loneliness until at the end of class Billy walked up.

"Sarah," he called. "You did that on purpose, didn't you?" "Yes," she replied, "I once wet my pants, too."

What is love? Love is unselfish compassion that preserves humanity. Sarah understood as a child, the pain inflicted by a conforming mass. She was a dissenter, even before the kids were allowed to gang up against Billy. She was relief.

What's Common?

Christopher Columbus was a dissenter. Frederick Douglas was a dissenter. Rosa Parks and Martin Luther King, Jr. were dissenters. The shepherd David was a dissenter. And yes, Sarah was a dissenter. They, by choice, represented the ones out of synchronization with the masses. They provided our world with relief.

Columbus, by his dissent, opened the door to the west, paving the way for freedom to worship, freedom to chose, freedom to grow, freedom to create, freedom to live in contentment.

Douglas, by his dissent, refusing the bonds of slavery, unshackled countless men, women, and children's conforming by law to an evil institution. His work, as a leader and abolitionist, found him employed later in life as U.S. Marshall for the District of Columbia. "No people who can produce a Douglas need despair," someone later remarked.

Parks' and Kings' dissent were in the spirit of justice spelled out in America's great documents. Their work to gain equal access, human dignity, and equality for all continues. David's dissent taught bravery, faith in God, and faith in self. Finally, Sarah's dissent epitomizes love and care for a fellow human.

In common, they were dissenters. Moreover, these dissenters were not afraid of standing alone. They were individualists as designed by the laws of nature. They were secure enough to stand and deliver for the good of humanity.

Negative Side of Dissent

The right to dissent can be taken too far. At this point, even if positive alignments are made, unifying the ones for peace, destructiveness becomes a looming result. Having no will to cooperate with humanity, will breach any respectable union we may have as a human family.

It's okay to disagree. However, some disagree because they are selfishly disagreeable people. Sour mouths, boiling with pain, anguish, intemperance, and hatred find it an art to disagree with anything and everything that may result in peace. We may disagree as to the color of a car, what is or what is not art, and what is or is not beauty. We can differ on what is a proper and healthy weight. But, again some go too far. They become reckless and unkind. They tend to be negative people full of complaints. They complain of the world's unwillingness to follow their ways demonstrated by their discomfort. Sinners, they cry out, demonizing workers for peace. They hate and find constant contentions with the liberal hearted. Many among those ranks evangelize hate. They are warriors. They will fight to promote agreement with their selfish, self-seeking, and self-promoting agendas.

I call for well thought-out and responsible dissent. I promote willingness to walk out of step with those whose practices are corrosive to the quilt of humanity. Upon this view is established the eighth law. If you are not willing to think on your own, tallying the sums of social, political, and religious thought, determining contributions to the harmony of humanity, I invite you to respect those who do. Others may not share your idealism and goals. Maybe they don't share the popular beliefs that you do. But, if we are to get along as a human family, we must respect the right to dissent.

Law Number One—Know and Respect Yourself

Law Number Two—Know and Respect Others

Law Number Three—Respect the Laws of Nature

Law Number Four—Appreciate the Mutual Design of Humanity

Law Number Five—Appreciate the Accomplishments and Intelligence of Others

Law Number Six—Be Honest, Never Patronizing

Law number Seven—Avoid Blanket Statements

Law Number Eight—Respect the Right To Dissent

17

Always Be Willing to Apologize
and
Ready to Forgive

Rule #9 in the *Commandments of Peace*

They sat there, father and daughter, as the movie came to a sentimental end. She looked up. As she did, she looked into her daddy's eyes. They were red stained, filled with water, and about to spill over. With every ounce of internal grit, he fought back, damming the flow. If, by chance, his finger would touch his eye, it would cause his well of feelings to overflow. This would create a stream contrary to his picture of manliness.

"Daddy," she said, as she pulled in tight. "I see it got you, too."

"What do ya mean?" was his gruff reply. He was still blinded in contention, not to show feeling.

"You've got tears in your eyes, too," she laughingly said as she tucked in closer, embracing his massive arm.

"No, I'm not!" Shrugging and wiggling his way free he explained, "It was the butter from the popcorn that irritated my eyes." He counseled her, "You ought to be careful not to put your hands in your face."

"I know," she replied as she sat up on the sofa. Reaching for the remote, to rewind the video, she said, calling out to her dad as he walked from the room, "It's all right to cry, too. I love you, Daddy." His voice, out of sight, responded, "I love you, too."

Many men, especially those so-called civilized men, have learned it is unmanly to drop a tear. When one does it brings into question his manliness. "Be a man!" We are taught, "Big boys don't cry." We are encouraged to be men not mice. In short, many of us are taught not to care, not to show compassion. In place of nature's law, which plays deep in our pockets of emotion, we establish ourselves as warriors. We are always right, and seldom wrong. When we are wrong, regardless the price, we are slow to admit it. Those who do are classified as weak. Naturally, we were designed with feelings. Our feelings in many ways communicate our conscious. Our conscious natures are backed with a consciousness tuned into an infinitive and natural balance of good and evil. When we rush through our daily activities, our inner ears are deafened. Less and less is heard internally, as we tune wider into the world around us.

Outwardly, we are swayed by the flawed and damaged. They too, have given themselves to habits contrary to nature's law. To many, the technical advancements of humans are greater than their concerns for humanity. More and more are magnetized by the things, created by mankind and desensitized to a natural call from within. This inner call preserves and protects humanity by the creation and sustaining of unity. Here is found respect. Our resistance to our inner selves has caused a breakdown in respect for humanity. Until this is realized in each of us, no religion or government can create an atmosphere of global peace. Peace is unity. Peace is cooperation. Our selfish leanings, bearing our communion with a flawed environment is corrosive to unity and a proven obstacle to cooperation. In this fractured state, peace is breached from the natural design of humanity.

Our abilities to apologize and forgive place us in direct competition with ourselves, as good and evil contend for inner-power. They are unsettling because somewhere in a constant and natural balance is a will to do what is right. When good wins, a healthy habit is formed. Humanity wins. When evil wins, our natural balance is thrown out of sync. Here is the foundation for bad habits.

The Need for Newness

It is our bad habits created of selfishness, that obstruct civility. It is civility that gives us manners. Manners are respect. There are few things in this world worse than the feeling of being disrespected. Humanity has come so far, that by our development of things we have out-paced ourselves.

We have learned by damming rivers, burning fuels, and trapping the sun's rays to harness power. By this, we can flip a switch and split asunder the darkness. We can power great medical centers for the healing of the sick and injured. We can light paths for travel at night. We can communicate over vast miles, sending and receiving information, speaking and hearing as if standing together. By use of this, ever-growing technological advance by mankind, we can remove the heat from summer and warm any wintry day. By this same power, we can shorten the life of a man sentenced to death. Little by little, slowly but surely, we have evolved a state of unrecognized interdependence. We may not want to realize it, but the more we discover and/or invent, the more we need each other. We need each other for service. We need each other for support. We need each other for developments to make secure our advancements.

If this theory of need is true, how it is we find so many at odds? Families are divided. Neighbors are isolated from each other. Communities are unconnected and nations are disunited. Many people find themselves in constant contention. But as complex as the controversies may be, a majority rest on the breaking of some of the laws of peace.

The laws of peace are really laws of respect. They begin with respect for self, followed by respect for others. They require healthy respect for nature and natural law, which is in constant enforcement. The respects found in the laws of peace are rules for courtesy.

When one of these commandments is broken, because they only serve to maintain unity, it is a very simple process to repair the break. Two sincere phrases, difficult to use, go far. They are "I'm sorry" and "I forgive." Use of these phrases requires a convincing and intelligent dose of humility but, somehow as we have evolved to the technological state of existence, we've lost our humble edge.

However, I believe deep in each of us, no matter how portentously snobbish or conceitedly pompous, is a constant glow of humility. On the back of tragedy, that glow becomes a fuel to the conscious. It empowers the good in us. It indefinitely places on hold our evil and divisive ways, until the crisis concludes. To get this healthy form of humility to come alive, we need renewal. Like nature's flow of seasons we need rebirth. In the areas above and below the equator, the further you go the more it is noticed, this natural flow.

At the end of each summer and the waves of heat, autumn comes. Here the earth is summoned to rest. The leaves lose their greenness giving way shades of gold, amber, and mirror the tones of a setting sun. The leaves fall from the trees. Soon as our bodies respond, we slow down to witness nature tucking in nature with a blanket of snow as life seemingly falls off to sleep.

But after a long rest, the blanket of snow is rolled back. Soon spring rings its alarm. The sun's rays reach below the earth's surface, shaking the seeds, waking the roots. As life is lifted from its sleepy state, the rain becomes a refreshing shower which readies nature to colorfully clothe itself in rainbows and uniforms of green. This is rebirth. This is renewal.

We have stayed the long nights partying with our inventions, intoxicated by our advances. Our minds are weary, we lack patience. We are hung over, tired, and unable to treat each other with respect. Our minds are cloudy. We are annoyed because as we look into others, we see images of ourselves. We are naturally reminded of our being out of sync with nature's laws. When we fail to tolerate others, it is because we can not tolerate ourselves. Nature has placed us at the point where we need each other. It is no accident that in

America if we want oranges, grapefruits, lemons, or limes, we need the states of Florida and California. If we need maple syrup, we need the New England states. If we need corn, wheat, and other grain, we need the west. We need, for many things the regions of our nation, but even more we need the world.

For coffee, we rely on South America. For bananas, we use Central America, for olives, we need the Mediterranean. For teas, we call on India and China. For gold, diamonds, platinum, titanium, as well as rich minerals, we rely on the nations of Africa. For fossil fuels, such as oil, we rely on imports from the Middle East.

There are many things that we rely on from the world, but in America we are blessed. Not all but, many of the foods and things that we get from the world can be produced right here at home. But, even here we need each other. Try to exist one day or even a fraction of a day without using the services of a fellow human. Unless you are exiled to a desert, buried in a cave, or left to wander, as beast through a forest, you will find your existence is well supported by your fellow humans.

Treat yourself with a newness of life. Try on nature's eyeglasses. Through them you will see below the surface of things that we are the same. Nature's vision penetrates the superficial world. It is blinded to the things that divide us: gender, race, age, religious and political alignments, economic and educational attainments. Clothing is no option to nature's laws; we are as naked the day we ventured from the womb. Nothing we attain conceals the human within.

Wake up! Like the nudging of spring, open your eyes. See the light, feel the warmth of the sun. Unwrap your hatreds and mistrusts. Rise up! Find someone different than you. Make a friend. Here and now, by our commitment to renewal, we can find hope. We can find unity. We can find social harmony. We can establish peace.

Apologizing and Forgiving

An apology is an admission of error or discourtesy given with an expression of regret. Apologizing is an act of recognition that the giver of such has caused someone pain or discomfort. An apology is like a medicine to the offended. But when given with an excuse, it's like rubbing salt or acid into a wound.

Forgiving is different, but closely related. To forgive is to make allowances that give room for error and weakness. A forgiver is a realist who understands that we, including self, are human and subject to misdeeds that inflict pain and undue pressures on others. The act of forgiving is an art. It allows one to simply put down the hurt, walk away from it, and move on with life. In the Lord's prayer, the practicing Christian is advised to forgive the trespasses and debts of others as the Lord forgives them. But forgiveness is not just a Christian thing. It is found attached and buried deep into every major religion that makes wise contact with the spirit of humanity.

There are two phrases in the English language that should be used more:

"I'm sorry" and "I forgive." Just as we are offended by others we, too, can be offensive. It is easy to react when we feel pain. Ask any patient in a dental office. However, it is hard to understand when we inflict pain. Ask any dentist. In this view is found the beauty of the Golden Rule:

"Do unto others as you would have them do unto you."

Treat others as you wish to be treated, allowing for imperfection. If you are careful to do so, you will begin to understand others. The superficials of age, sex, race, and education, politics and religion, will fall, leaving naked the soul, no different in construction than your own. Here people are treated as people. Here natural law values us the same. Here is the sincere apology when you are mistreated. Here is the powerhouse of forgiveness. Here is the concern for others that promotes an apology.

Wisdom is not knowledge. Wisdom is the use of power gathered from knowledge. Knowledge is gained by our personal experience. Due to our personal experiences, we may not understand the complaints of wrongs against others. Not feeling the pains and pressure we cause, does not indicate they do not exist. They do and they hurt. Many times we are found loitering at the root. Here we work assiduously keeping victims uneased. In this is found the germ that creates the virus that infects and sentences the undiagnosed to a death of intolerance. Here is the disease of hate.

In many cases the virus of evil that destroys one's immunity to hatred and renders the victim intolerant, has no cure. However the infection can be prevented. It can be prevented by the application of an apology when put on notice that a wrong has been committed. A simple, I am sorry, can go a long way as a medicine salving the wound to the human family.

More on Forgiveness

The maintenance of health, within the human family requires a healthy dose of apologizing and forgiving. Quite a bit has been shared on the act of apologizing, but now let us focus more on forgiving. Only half of the regimen is completed by apologizing. The other half requires the action of the recipient. The act required is forgiveness.

Alexander Pope, in the essay on criticism wrote, "to err is human, to forgive divine." Forgiveness is difficult. It is difficult because it is held tight by the level of pain. The most foolish advice ever shared is "to forgive and forget." How does one truly forget? The trauma of a wrong leaves embedded in the memory a scar. The size of the scar is commensurate with the level of offense and ones personal experience.

"Come on, forget it, let's bury the hatchet," we are told. It would be nice if we could move on and forget misdeeds. However, we must face facts. It is rare for a man to bury a hatchet and forget where it is. If we were to bury hatchets, by forgetting wrongs committed, we would also bury our memories of shortcomings, trespasses, debts, and wrongs inflicted. We would hide from our knowledge the pains and stresses associated with them. This would void our concerns for others and give rise to continuing injustice.

Can You Really Forgive and Forget?

When I was a boy of 12, I lived across the street from my grandparents. At this age, I enjoyed bike riding. I would ride for hours. Mile after mile I would travel. Seemingly, the days had no end. I was a kid at peace. I was larger than the world and free. I was free to think and free to imagine. One day, my visit at my grandparents brought my biking to an end.

My brother, Emory, and I were sitting out one summer day on grandparent's patio, part of which I helped Granddaddy build. It was hot outside! Granddaddy loved it that way. For some reason he enjoyed the sweltering heat. His house was not air conditioned. He had a little window unit installed in Grandma's room. But for him, he was more interested in having me cover his storm windows with plastic to lock out the draft. Frequently, I would tease Granddaddy about the heat. I would compare him to the Hebrew boys, Shadrach, Meshach, and Abednego and their visit in the fiery furnace. I would tell my brothers the reason Granddaddy was a saint was because he kept it too hot for the devil to take up residence.

Forgetting his love affair with the heat, I found very few people as kind and wise as him. Some cousins and close friends did not see my grandfather this way. They lacked the intimate relationship that I had. This relationship reached through the crude, seemingly uneducated, lump of coal and found nestled inside a diamond, perfectly sparkling, with wisdom clear with love. It was his humor, in the form of teasing, that brought my bike riding to a halt.

Emory and I sat out on that patio that day eating a refreshing, sweet, and cold watermelon. Grandma served it to us as we shared some time with Granddaddy. That juice from the pieces of melon was splashing and dripping as my brother and I washed our faces in it. To stop the juice from running onto my clothes I moved out into the grass. This positioned me to witness the start of trouble.

Horseplay it was. Grandma had told us to stop horseplaying. But, we were boys and that day Granddaddy was, too. As he neared the completion of his treat, I watched him look up. Those eyes, that smile signaled mischief. That was it. The melon was gone. Granddaddy finished his, Emory was still eating. Granddaddy moved in close. Emory was unsuspecting, his head still buried in the melon. I, too, had finished, although I pretended to continue eating, while spying what was about to happen.

Casplashhh! Right down Emory's back the juice poured. Granddaddy washed his rind right across my brother's back. After the shock and laughs, Emory settled back into eating. I could see in his eye the calculating of devilment. The melon was gone. He, too, pretended to continue to eat hoping to catch Granddaddy off guard. Like a bolt of lightning, that brother of mine leaped out of his seat and lunged towards an unsuspecting Grandfather. Casplashhh! Emory covered his head with his hollowed out rind. This was the first time I had ever seen his head covered with anything other than a hat. If he ever had hair on top, it was before I was born. Granddaddy jumped up with his new melon helmet, face drenched in melon juice and sounded the battle cry, "Get'em, Donny!"

Emory had already rounded the house once before I had stopped laughing to join the chase. Round and around that house we went, passing Granddaddy, as he limped along laughing.

"CATCH him Donny, catch him!" he yelled. Granddaddy loved gardening. In the back of his home was a large vegetable garden bordered with flowers. Along the side, Granddaddy grew the prettiest rose bushes you would ever want to see. He would stake the bushes to keep them growing straight. His stakes were crude. They were nothing from the hardware store. The old man was a recycler before recycling was popular. He tied his roses to old discarded galvanized steel and aluminum pipes that he hammered into the ground.

As Emory ran, he dodged in and out, weaving between the rose bushes. I was smart. My chase was scientific. I knew the shortest distance between two points was a straight line. I jumped the bushes. The last jump left my leg impaled on a stake. Five inches of torn flesh next to my knee was open to the bone. I hopped over to the patio. By this time, Grandma had come out. Surprisingly she gave no speech, didn't say, "I told you so." She patiently walked into the house. She returned with a bottle of isopropyl rubbing alcohol. Without a word, she delivered a splash to my leg. Surprisingly I felt no burn, no sting, no pain, not even an itch. The crack team of physicians moved in. Grandma, Granddaddy, and Emory examined the wound. The prognosis was serious. Plan of action; call Daddy. Quick!

By the time my father arrived, some of the flesh moved together. It still required further action, so off to the emergency room. The doctor came in. He probed the open wound with a tongue depressor. Still no feeling. Another technician came in and washed it out. The doctor returned and he sewed me back together. A tetanus shot, same bandages, and I went home.

The next day the pain paid me a visit. Below the bandage, an itch developed I could not reach. My bike riding had come to an end. How stupid we were. But we did have fun. What does my story have to do with forgiving and forgetting? Everything!

Years have passed. My wound has healed. Now and then I take a ride on my bike. With the exception of a scar, I am 100% well. The scar is a reminder. It reminds me that time heals wounds. It reminds me that wounds leave scars. It reminds me to be careful. Each time I notice my scar, I reckoned with insight into the human family. Engraved is a lesson about life.

We can forgive, but we do not forget. We simply limit our focus and move on. The wise never dwell on who or what has wronged them. The wise never forget. Neither do they explode with rage about the transgressions and trespass of others. They isolate the offense and when the bandage of apology is applied, they offer forgiveness. The wound may scar, but, to the wise, the scar is valued as experience. By our personal choosing, our experiences help or hurt us. They help if the game of life continues in play. They hurt, if we succumb to the possible aggravations they present. The ninth law in the *Rules for Peace* is a means by which we keep the game in play. Always be willing to apologize and be ready to forgive.

Two seldom-used phrases in the English language are, "I'm sorry" and "I forgive." Just as we are offended by others, we too offend. It is easy to react when we feel pain. It is hard to understand when we inflict pain. Here is the beauty of the Golden Rule: "Do unto others as you would have done unto you."

If you follow this advice you can't go wrong bringing healing to the human family.

Law Number One—Know and Respect Yourself

Law Number Two—Know and Respect Others

Law Number Three—Respect the Laws of Nature

Law Number Four—Appreciate the Mutual Design of Humanity

Law Number Five—Appreciate the Accomplishments and Intelligence of Others

Law Number Six—Be Honest, Never Patronizing

Law Number Seven—Avoid Blanket Statements

Law Number Eight—Respect the Right To Dissent

Law Number Nine—Always Be Willing to Apologize and Ready to Forgive

18

Take Time to Rest

Rule #10 in the *Commandments of Peace*

Here is a simple story, but true. When I was a boy, my mother bought me a watch. She advised me not to wind it too tight. Somehow, I did just what she warned me not to and it broke. It's that simple. It broke. I'm a big boy now. Today, I wear, when I do, a gold Longines watch. It, too, is an old wind-up, an antique. I am very careful, so very careful, not to wind it too tight.

That's the story of my watch. Other than my watch, we had many wind-up things. My father even speaks of a wind-up car. He said when he was younger he had some kind of car he had to wind up by crank to start. He told stories about people having problems with the crank. If the person failed to remove the crank and jump out of the way the motor would force the crank to turn backward. This contributed to more than a few headaches and concussions.

We had many wind-up things when we were growing up. For one, we had a wind up alarm clock. I never understood why. Our sleeping, schooling, and working patterns never really allowed us use of an alarm clock. My dad and I were light sleepers. We would wake up at the slightest sound. We all managed to wake up in time for school and work. When we did over sleep, daddy would nudge our feet and clue is in that morning had split asunder the skies. Today, my wife will witness that I still don't use alarm clocks.

We had toys that required winding up. The majority of them were easily broken. The cars wouldn't run. The robots wouldn't walk. A lot of these toys were previously used. By the time we got a lot of them, they were in a mistreated and injured state. I remember my mother bringing home a music box one day. It was nice. It was sort of like a radio with one station and one song. Over and over, it would play the same tune. It was a matter of time until that, too, broke.

My mother did "days work," as she called it. She would go out and clean homes for people as a way of earning extra cash. Now and then some of her employers would get rid of things. Some even did so in lieu of payment for her services. They called it bartering. I called it disrespect. Especially, when the trade contained things that had long since lost their use. Similar to the wind up things were things that required pulling strings. Usually, they were dolls.

The wind up and pull string concepts in gadgets were soon replaced by battery powered novelties. Even they would run down. Even they became dysfunctional.

Tugging and Warring

People are no different. We are wound up daily by a constant influx of news reports. Much of it is negative. Day to day, we allow our strings to be pulled by our family, our friends, our employers, and fads alike. Our mental batteries are routinely overcharged by advertisers of religious and political thoughts. Daily, through a barrage of methods, we are fired upon by religious and political groupings who narrow-mindedly campaign for our support and crusade for our dollars.

Both the religious and the political seemingly converge upon the pinnacle of nonsense as they promote immeasurable statistics and claims. While they may not represent mainstream thought, held by the sober practitioner of religion or the dispassionate but honest patriot, they represent a fringe element of intolerance misinformed but well-intentioned group of bigots. Many who silently watch from the sidelines are turned off by their pageantry of ignorance and unbalanced conclusions. Two issues burning the religious and political streets of America are abortion and prayer in schools. Both issues are really non-issues. It is my belief that both are matter of choice.

First abortion. I am and forever will be, as far as my understanding will allow, pro-life. I believe that life begins at the moment of conception. I believe that the sanctity of life deserves my utmost respect and protection. Yet, I also understand others do not believe as I do. Some believe that life truly begins with the development of internal organs, such as the heart and brain. Still others believe life truly starts at birth. With a sobriety of Christian ethics and prayer, I respect a well informed woman's right to choose. This is an issue consciously respected by the U.S. Constitution, upheld by the U.S. Supreme Court, and sworn by oath to be protected by the chief executive officer, the President of the United States of America. Maybe rather than complain about the second non-issue, prayer in schools, they should spend more time in prayer. Prayer is an act of communion with God. It is spiritual. Prayer should be an open communication faxed from one's heart and soul to God and God alone. Yes, the U.S. Supreme Court banned Bible readings and organized prayer in school, but they did not ban prayer. Prayer is a matter of personal choice. It is a right and unencumbered choice of an individual. Sanctioned or not, the right of a student to pray in a public school has never been abridged.

These two issues are glaring examples of uninformed, misguided, and deranged thought. They are weighty issues of gratuitous stress that, if replaced by a healthy concern for peace and justice, would serve to unify and make peaceful our homes and world.

Regularly, we are also preyed upon by separatists, many of whom resemble us. They are also wolves who selfishly attempt to control of individuals who feel bypassed, ignored, and left on the sidelines of society. They create factions that oppose tolerance and diversity in our society. It has become common that minds are steered into prejudice, chauvinism, and bigotry, some to the point of no return.

Every day, every way, and everybody seems to be pulling in this tug-of-war. It is hard, at best to find peace. It is even harder to find peace of mind. It is too loud, too harsh, too fast, and too hot. Round and round we spin day after day, fitting in and not fitting in. The tide of fads is high as the waves roll in giving the latest, "What's in? What's out? What's hot? What's cold?"

We are awake, but forced into a stuporous sleep of intoxicated indifference. We sluggishly slide, drag, and shuffle each second in life toward death. If life is to be enjoyed, we must slow down. We must end the tugging and warring. We must find ourselves. We must take a rest.

Perpetual Motion?

Some things are constant. For example, the sun shines. The earth rotates as it revolves around the sun. The moon orbits its path like every other planet. But even the reach of the sun, radiating our earth with a blanket of warmth and light, is compromised as clouds move in to shower and refresh the land. Here even nature requires rest. Naturally night falls, giving rest to day. The season of summer prepares for rest of autumn. Repose is found when nature safely tucks in autumn with a blanket of winter. The tides rise and fall. Change is a natural or forced movement from one state of existence to another. Rest is the act of seeking calm from an excited state. Perpetual motion is different in that it is constant. Perpetual motion is a concept of a system that, on its own, could operate indefinitely, once started, void of any additional outside energy. It is believed that such a system lacks agreement with the proper and tested laws of physics. Anything set into motion will run down if left to itself. Human beings are no different.

Humans are wound up at conception; the strings are pulled at birth; the first gasp of air breathed beyond the womb is charged to power us until we take our final rest.

The mind, the body, the soul or spirit of mankind is like the strongest, well-oiled machine. When machinery runs, friction is created. Friction creates heat. Heat causes entropy. Entropy is a process of degradation, or running down, set in motion by time in use. This time use is the measure of wear. Entropy is irreversible. This irreversible condition ruins the quality of life and life expectancy of the machine in use. Unlike machines which can be shut off, the mind is in constant use. This use can be involuntary, such as our dreaming at night. The constant movement of the mind by guilt, apprehension, doubt, fear, anxiety, are stressful and mentally strenuous activities.

I call this mental toil "mental friction." Being mentally frictioned is being over-heated and open to the effects of entropy. The mind quickens the process of deterioration. Whether conscious or unconscious, the mind is constantly under attack by stress.

The body, too, is under constant attack. First, it is attacked by heredity. Some bad genes were traded at conception. This trade into cell structure delivers a broad range of results. Some people are restrained by weakened cardiovascular systems. Others live in arthritic and rheumatoid pain as skeletal joints are challenged. Neuralgia, bone and muscle aches weaken many who would otherwise be strong. Yet for others, heredity results in poor eyesight, impaired hearing, and a host of other unearned physical conditions. Unnaturally, by the overindulgence of vices, such as overeating, smoking, consumption of alcohol and narcotics, many have contributed to their own physical demise. The momentary self gratification of the senses by artificial means, as through the use of depressants, stimulants, or anything that counterfeits the body's relationship to the laws of nature, holds the body at bay and promotes stress. This stress is unhealthy and motivates deterioration.

Spiritually, the soul of existence in human beings is an area understudied. Here are the invisible alignments with positive and negative forces. Here infinite knowledge is traded. Here our affiliation with the world around us draws out influences that excite or depress our natures. Our constant wins and losses, our achievements, our victories, set-backs, defeats, excitement, and depression, tax and toil us. Our spiritual development directly relates to our mental and physical development. A strong spirit makes for a healthy and mentally happy individual. A weak spirit is an open door to sickness and mental despondency.

The mind, the body, the spirit must be protected. Other than the natural glow of the sun, nothing and no one has developed into a perpetual state. We need rest. The lack of quality rest is chasing the existence of living matter into retreat. Death is the outcome. Natural law has found no match for its power. We must find rest.

What's Annoying You?

Annoyance can be productive. The man once annoyed by dragging a palate from place to place, as he transported his wares, was relieved when his annoyance resulted in the creation of the wheel. He was even more relieved when he learned two wheels were better than one.

Think about this: that man who was annoyed by pushing and pulling his cart up hills was relieved when his annoyance resulted in the use of animals for pulling and pushing power. He was even more relieved when he found it better to use a beast than a bird.

Think about this: that man, having to fetch camels, mules, donkeys, oxen, and horses, for the work of pulling pushing was relieved when his annoyance resulted in the creation of a motor to replace animal use. He was even more relieved with the development of a steering wheel.

Think about it! From this point, annoyance after annoyance and the discomforts associated with them have created millions upon millions of inventions. The inventions and devices resulting from our annoyances pad our lives with comfort and convenience. Socially, we often find ourselves annoyed. This too is productive when it results in a constructive advance for humanity. Daily, the barrage of information, coupled with our heritage of mistrust among people keeps us alert and ready for combative interaction. This excited state is the most common obstacle to peace.

We want walls. We want laws. We want protection from people we fear. Hyper, as if prompted by an overdose of nicotine and caffeine, we want weapons readied for action. If visitors were to drop by from distant galaxies, our number one goal would be to declare war. Why are we so excited? Why are we so negatively hyper in our relationships with each other? We need rest.

Take Time to Rest

This is the last but important law in the commandments of peace. Take time to rest. Stop! Relax! Tune out the rigid and hyper sounds of life. Ask yourself *why?* Why are we so filled with negative energy? Why are we so ready to war? Who are the people we are ready to battle? What personal thing have they done? Slow down! Think! Other than those who resemble your features, who do you know that you can call a friend?

Calm down! Listen to the soft and harmonious music of nature. Close your eyes and imagine. Imagine what a beautiful world this would be if we could only learn to get along. Imagine us giving peace a chance. Imagine neighbor helping neighbor. Imagine opportunity for all regardless of sex, race, religious, or political background. Imagine churches promoting faith over religion. Imagine children happy and healthy, enjoying life as they grow into our future. Imagine the sick getting quality medical attention regardless of their economic state. Imagine freedom to live as you choose as long as you don't trample or encroach upon the freedoms of others. Imagine no greed, no hunger, then think.

What can you do to contribute to a better community? What can your community do to contribute to a better city or town? What can your city or town do to contribute to a better county? What can your county do to contribute to a better state? What can your state do to promote a better nation and contribute to a more perfect union? What can this nation do to contribute to a better world?

International trade and commerce is good, but what is it in a background of chaos and hate? National pride is good, but how can one be proud of a nation which allows children to go to sleep with stomachs aching from hunger? Peace does not begin with law. Peace begins with the individual. How can we rid ourselves of unemployment in a nation where sexism and racism are rampant? When will we all begin to judge people on their content of character? Rest and imagine giving peace a chance.

When I invite you to rest, I am not inviting you to sleep. Sleep is natural. Sleep is the periodic suspension of consciousness during which the powers of the body are restored. I am inviting all to relax. Relax by stepping back and calming down. Re-evaluate your contribution to peace. Examine your personal hold on peace. Examine your fears and anxieties. Evaluate your trust. Are you fearful of people you have never met? How do these people differ from you? One thing I have found in life, we all have deep within us a desire for peace. But it is hampered by past injustices, misunderstandings, trespasses, and prejudices by misinformation shared by bigoted creatures of hate. We need to back off and examine our contributions to peace. We must give peace a chance.

We are at full alert. Constantly, by habit, many of us have learned to see life only through our eyes. The time is now to begin understanding, our vision may be distorted. Our learned tendencies of prejudice and human neglect have dimmed our abilities to understand and feel the pain of others. This is because we ourselves are so bottled up with hurt, disappointment, and feelings of inferiority. In order to take pride in ourselves, we have learned to put down others. We do this freely with selfish excitement. We need to rest.

Sleep may restore the body, but how can one sleep with the mind overtaxed and a spirit exhausted? Sleeplessness is a by-product of a negatively excited life. Sleeping does not allow conscious examination of one's personal and intelligent contribution to peace. Rest does. Rest allows a relaxing of the mind, body, and spirit. Rest is about taking a break.

Now and then, when the temper is raised and the heart is at full speed, flooding the body with adrenaline and your irrational views are supported by your anger, loosen up. Release your hands. Relax your muscles. Take an intermission to examine your contribution to peace. Rest! We spend too much time fighting obstacles in our search for peace. Give peace a chance. Take time to think. Take time to rest.

Law Number One—Know and Respect Yourself

Law Number Two—Know and Respect Others

Law Number Three—Respect the Laws of Nature

Law Number Four—Appreciate the Mutual Design of Humanity

Law Number Five—Appreciate the Accomplishments and Intelligence of Others

Law Number Six—Be Honest, Never Patronizing

Law Number Seven—Avoid Blanket Statements

Law Number Eight—Respect the Right to Dissent

Law Number Nine—Always Be Willing to Apologize and Ready to Forgive

Law Number Ten—Take Time to Rest

19

Natural Law

Just What Is It ?

Throughout this book, I have referred to Natural Law. Chapter eleven was devoted to the third law in the *Ten Commandments of Peace.* You, the reader, are now and forever challenged to, "Respect the Laws of Nature." It is about respecting Natural Law. Natural law that I refer to is what keeps the sun alive and glowing. It keeps the earth rotating and the stars and planets positioned in space. By this same law of cosmic proportions, I believe our interactions within the human level are ordered.

Natural Law supersedes man-made law. Man-made law is an order of rules set up by governmental authorities. Here man-made rules govern the transactions and interactions between individuals and groups of individuals. Man-made law is a random law which constantly changes. It is randomly adapting and usually bears the prejudice, naive ignorance, selfishness, mistrust, discontent, imperfection, and self-interest of its authors. By what other reason could one explain amendments?

Thomas Hobbes and John Locke, 17th century English philosophers, introduced an original state of nature out of which a social contract arose and combined this theory with Natural Law. Locke's doctrine that, naturally, we are endowed with certain inalienable rights that cannot be abrogated by any governing authority is recognized, respected, and noted in the United States Declaration of Independence as: "among the Powers of the Earth the separate and equal Station to which the Laws of Nature and of Nature's God entitle them . . . We hold these truths to be self evident, that all Men [People] are created equal," and "that they are endowed by their Creator with certain unalienable Rights that among them are Life, Liberty and the Pursuit of Happiness."

In these words are embodied the reach of Natural Law that is yours for the asking.

The ancient Greek philosophers are documented as the first to present a Natural Law doctrine. Heraclitus, in the 6th century B.C., spoke of a common wisdom that controls the universe, "for all human laws are nourished by one, the divine." Aristotle distinguished:

> A rule of justice is natural that has the same validity everywhere, and does not depend on our accepting it or not; a rule is legal that, in the first instance, may be settled in one way or the other indifferently.

The Stoics, especially the philosopher Chrysippus of Soli, (25 B.C.) developed a systematic Natural Law theory. Stoicism teaches that the whole cosmos is rationally ordered by an active principle variously man-made (God, mind, or fate). Every individual nature is relative to the cosmos. To live virtuously means to live in accord with one's nature and right reason. This doctrine was popularized by the Romans who taught that wise individual seeks to consciously embrace the rational life. Cicero, the great 1st century B.C. orator, spoke of a Natural Law definition in his DeRepublica as:

> True law is right reason in agreement with nature; it is of universal application, unchanging and everlasting; it summons to duty by it commands, and averts from wrongdoing by its prohibitions . . . There will not be different laws at Rome and at Athens, or different laws now and in the future, but one eternal and unchangeable law will be valid for all nations and for all times.

Christians found the Natural Law doctrine of the Stoics quite compatible with their beliefs. St. Paul, a Jew by birth and the most published Biblio-Christian philosopher, spoke of Gentiles (non-Jews), who do not have the Mosaic Law, "by nature what the law requires." (Romans 2:14)

St. Isidore, the 6th century A.D. Spanish theologian of Seville, declared that Natural Law is observed everywhere by natural instinct; he cited as illustrations the laws of marriage and the procreation of children.

In the *Summa Theologiae* (Summary Treatise of Theology, 1265-73 A.D.), St. Thomas Aquinas called the rational guidance of creation by God the "Eternal Law." The eternal law gives all beings the inclination to those actions and aims that are proper to them. Rational creatures, by directing their own actions and guiding the actions of others, share in divine reason itself. "This participation in the Eternal Law by rational creature is called the Natural Law." Its dictates correspond to the basic inclinations of human nature. Thus, according to Aquinas, it is possible to distinguish good from evil by the natural light of reason.

Natural Law is perfect absolution theory in practice. It is absolute because it requires no amendments or addenda. It is perfect because over the centuries, it has proved to be consistent. Natural Law is universal law. This type of law permeates every geographical boundary. It is branded naturally upon the heart and searing the soul and spirit of humanity. Natural Law is a body of universally instinctive principles derived from nature and binding upon the human society in the absence of, or in addition to, man-made law. The rules that govern the positioning of the universe are the same body of stationary rules enacted to conduct the behavior of the nucleus nestled in the atom. To Natural Law, we are no match.

Natural Law is cosmic law. Natural law is considered fundamentally unchanging, and universally applicable. It is infinite, exact and offers no excuses, or apologies for its acts. Natural Law is a Divine arrangement set into motion with time.

When we supernaturally tap into its guidance, we are mysteriously lifted to a spiritual realm far distant above the limits of ordinary human thought. Upon this level, we are challenged to be superhuman. We are called to be ambassadors of peace.

This may be your *One Last Call.*

20

Why We Can't Wait

Please read this chapter completely. Because of your being predisposed to certain prejudices, you may think to stop reading at certain points. You just may be the person to which this chapter appeals. I challenge you to consider patiently and soberly the stories of reality. My only appeal is that you join with me on a journey, an upward climb, toward being the best that the natural and infinite forces our Creator intended you to be. These words may, with your help, change this nation. We may be moved to legitimately position ourselves as the truly greatest example of peace and prosperity. America, with its diversities representing every variance of humanity, is a microcosm of the world. If we can make it, the world can make it. It is my belief we can. With your effort and mine we will.

My Prologue

I was born a descendant of African-American heritage. In my blood flows the rich extraction of Europe, Native America, and the continent of Africa. It was not my choice to be born. It was not my choice to have this hereditary combination. But I had no choice. I was born the proud son of Francis and Elaine Harris. By this union is found the descendant of a U.S. President, a Native American, and a slave. My roots were traced back years ago. We already had knowledge of Caucasians and Native Americans, being part of a racial equation on my mother's side. But we were shocked, when we learned that one such person was the author of a document that many years later would serve to defend the rights of his illegitimate, but real grandson. His name, Thomas Jefferson. Jefferson was a revolutionary leader, political philosopher, U.S. President, and author of the Declaration of Independence.

President Jefferson was a member of the Continental Congress, Chairman of the committee that prepared the Declaration of Independence, U.S. minister to France, U.S. secretary of State, and once leader of the Democratic Republican Party. I thought, in some ways, the parties sounded alike. Today the Democrats and Republicans both direct the nation. These two parties find roots in a once-unified era whose leader wrote, in his first draft declaring the sovereignty and independence of this nation:

> We hold these truths to be self-evident:
> that all men are created equal; that
> they are endowed by their creator with
> inherent and inalienable rights;
> that among these are life, liberty and
> the pursuit of happiness.

The words of Jefferson's early draft had the words "with inherent and inalienable rights." It was the Continental Congress that revised it to read, "with certain inalienable rights." These words are the guarantees of personal liberty. The framers, representing this new nation, would "rather be exposed to the inconveniences attending too much liberty than . . . too small a degree of it." The words of liberty drafted on the American check to be drawn upon by it citizens, later defined by the fourteenth amendment to the U.S. Constitution, from the bank of justice. Jefferson wrote in 1787, "The tree of liberty must be refreshed from time to time with the blood of 'patriots and tyrants. It is its natural manure." Who could be any more patriotic than the soldiers of liberty and justice? John and Robert Kennedy, Medgar Evers, Martin Luther King, Jr. and Malcolm X, who, near the end of his life, learned of the beauty and humanhood of all people, regardless of their race reached out for America's promise. Rosa Parks, the mother of the civil rights movement, fades into the shadow of people, of all races, who stood up for justice and fairness and Black mothers, fathers, brothers, sisters, grandparents, children, clergymen, teachers, and others were hosed down in the streets of Birmingham, as a nation stood by inactive.

The word was out, a politically powerful ancestor of a boy born American, but denied by the color of his skin, had left the door unguarded to the promise granted by his creators. By creation, a distant grandson, removed from the throne of respect, was endowed with the inalienable rights of life, liberty, and the pursuit of happiness. Inalienable rights are supreme rights carved into the permanent rock of natural law. Man-made law may rule from time to time with unfairness, but soon it is judged in the courts of nature and found naturally unconstitutional.

American patriotic songs are about personal peace and communal peace. Real freedom is finding peace. Peace is truth and justice woven together in a fabric of fairness. Yes, liberty, is enriched by the blood of patriots. The patriots of the American Civil Rights movement were the martyrs whose blood still flows on the conscience of a nation called to make real a dream of sister- and brotherhood. Sadly, it is also the nightmarish blood of tyrants that remind us the roots of liberty are being deprived.

Many times, the example of Adolf Hitler is used to depict this madness depriving the life giving food of respect to liberty. While Hitler was a mad tyrant, steeped in the vile mixtures of prejudice, bigotry, and chauvinism, he was not American. He was a fascist. We Americans fought against fascism. But, in America today is a new form of fascism. This new clean-cut form is disguised by the rhetoric of moralists who preach faithfulness to the family, yet are on second and third marriages. They preach safety and toughness on crime, but find much grief standing behind policemen who walks on moral ground, keeping our cities safe. With ease, such politicians support law officials who are motivated by racism and sexism.

The new fascist is a wolf which follows no Judeo-Christian ethic, void of the lessons of love and respect for all humanity. The new fascist claims to be a fighter for workers rights who nevertheless opposes labor unions, once formed to empower the worker. The new fascists are uptight with the idea of multiculturalism. The new fascists are bloodthirsty partisans who wedge open, divide us, and pit us against each other. They speak of the evils of government. Sadly, they represent the government. They design and promote political thought. By their lead, groups of hatred and intolerance are formed. They are formed merely from fear. It is a fear of minorities and an unwillingness to share the opportunities of wealth and power. It is the fear of immigration and the birth of immigrant children on our shores. If you don't believe we are divided by more than principle alone, I invite you to examine the platforms of the 1996 Political Party conventions. Look into the make-up of the militia movements. Examine if you will, the Farakans. But, if you do, check out the Dukes, Buchanans, Gingrichs, and their messages as well.

Let's go back to the good old days. Let's go back to a time when Americans had values. Let's go back to a time when education was meaningful. Let's go back to the day when people showed respect and courtesy. There was a time when the dollar had value. There was a time when the people had a healthy respect for the law. Let's change our judicial system. Let's go back.

For many, a trip back in time would be a great adventure. For others, a trip back in time would be a bewildering trap of terror. The days in America were periodically the worst humanity had to offer. America may have had values, but those values were cheapened when they devalued the worth of a people whose ancestors, for the most part, were participants in a dream for a better life as they flooded our nations shores of opportunity. Some ancestors were sold, stolen, raped and ripped from fields and sucking breast to become unwillful participants in America's worst and evil past of slavery. The freedoms realized by African-Americans, in particular, are evolving freedoms. These freedoms evolved slowly over the past one hundred and fifty years. These freedoms are the result of war, protest, and constant begging for human respect and dignity. There were days, old days, when education was meaningful, but meaningful to whom? Beyond reading, writing, and arithmetic in segregated public schools and private schools, as scores of parochial schools were set up to counter act the 1954 Supreme Court ruling that declared separate but equal systems of public education unconstitutional. What was taught, even passively, other than the superiority of one people and the inferiority of another?

Let's go back to the days of people showing respect and courtesy and witness African-American soldiers returning from war, having aided in the victory of our nation, only to find a lack of opportunity or signs reading "White only" as they sought lodging and a hot meal. These men were the real eyewitnesses of America at its worst as their brothers and sisters of race were hosed down, beaten, and ravaged by dogs in the streets of Birmingham, Alabama, as nation stood idly by.

Let's go back to the days when the dollar had value. Perhaps it did, but there were days when so few of those dollars were seen in the African American community trapped by an invisible army cut off by an invisible economic embargo made real by discrimination. There was a time when there was a healthy respect for the law. However, that respect failed many times to understand the lawlessness of officers who sought by force to maintain an infamously crude, mean-spirited, vulgar, and contemptible status quo.

Let's change our judicial system. This has been the cry of many Americans, after the mock justice displayed during the Simpson trial. But, where were these voices after the Simi-Valley trials of four officers, caught on tape, mercilessly beating an unarmed man? Where were these voices when the assassin of Medgar Evers was repeatedly found not guilty? Where are the voices seeking changes in our judicial system as courts are transformed into kangaroo courts, as scores of men are statistically judged and sentenced more harshly on the basis of skin color alone? Let's go back when?

We can do better! Our best days are not behind us. Our best days are yet to come. They are coming.

My Story

My story is my marriage to a beautiful descendant of German extraction. My wife hales from a typical American family of seven. Recently, her sister married one of the finest young men in America. Prior to the nuptials, we had the traditional bachelor's party. I in the company of his friends and relatives, had come together for the party. The party started off cool. Bit by bit, it warmed into a stupidly irresponsible, but innocent and fun-filled evening of excitement. As I witnessed the over-indulgence of alcohol intoxicating and trashing a soon-sleeping groom, I had to smile. We had gone bar hopping when the groom-to-be declared, "Donnell . . . I am drunk." He was. He staggered away, out of sight.

I walked through the bar looking for him. I asked his friends. I checked the bathroom; perhaps he was sick. A groomsman then told me that he was in the van. We had rented a van to responsibly transport us that night. I went out and checked the van. Sure enough, he was engulfed in a sleep that only the powers of the universe could have removed. I returned to the bar.

As I walked across the floor, I was stopped by one of the guys in the party. "So, let me get this straight. You are married to his girlfriend's sister?"

"Yes," I gave my cautioned reply. I had seen these mannerisms before and heard this type of inflection in the voice. The face did not show camaraderie, rather it was the look of confrontation.

"You married a White girl?" he asked.

"Yes."

"Well, I just want you to know you won't be welcomed where we come from." Knowing the history of certain cities and the large number of people that became members in the Ku Klux Klan, a fraternal order of some kind in the brotherhood of White men. I replied, "If I weren't married to her, I may not have been welcomed."

"No, I don't want to sound prejudiced. You know, I once wanted to do a Black girl. Don't you two find it difficult dealing with people?"

"Not really. Our difficulties come from negative people steeped in ignorance. We don't surround ourselves with people like that. So I guess we don't find it difficult. We both come from two very good families."

On another occasion, I was standing in my in-law's home when a neighbor kid innocently asked if I knew White people were smarter than Black people? I asked where he learned this. He quickly responded, everybody knew it. Little did he know everybody in that house was familiar with MD route #665. This route, one of the major entryways and exits of one of the major cities and once capitol of the United States where General George Washington resigned his commission before the 1st Constitutional President of the United States of America, Annapolis. Route 665 was named after a Medical Doctor State Senator and National Secretary of the Republican party, Aris T. Allen. Those present also knew, that neither of his parents had the determination or patience to complete high school.

My story is the story of experience. It is the direct experience of confrontation. It is personal confrontation which represents the conflicts of a society weakened by the powers of prejudice, the badness of bigotry, and the crime of chauvinism. My life has been and continues to be a microcosm of the world around me.

We all have life stories. Some stories stick out, such as, the first time we were really scared, the first bike, the first day of school, or the first kiss of love. Most experiences that stick out are those that excite or depress the emotions. They are the experiences that make you warm and tingly giving rise to goosebumps. Or those that anger or promote that flow of tears. For many, these stories of life that really stick out are systematically repeated. These stories are the sometimes funny, usually painful, stories of pressure and grief brought on by a social environment to judge people on the basis of exterior qualities alone.

My story is a story of challenge. It is challenge developed
into a goal. My goal is to encourage and invite, first my
nation, then my world, on a continuous journey of peace.
There is one thing that I truly believe we all have in common,
that is a desire to live in a world at peace. At least, I hope
everyone desires that. I further believe that systematic employing of the *Ten Commandments of Peace* by individuals will
promote peace.

Conflict and war promote and sustain the wealth of a
handful of individuals who for their own selfish enrichment
by pecuniary gain instigate conflict. We should be suspicious
of those disposed to choose war to resolve conflicts. From the
earliest ages we, especially Americans, most of European
descent, have chosen violence as a means to subdue dissi-
dents. It has become a means by which the underclass and
minority males have chosen to obtain opportunity, parity, and
an economic foothold in the climb from poverty to comfort.
Reducing the propensity to war and violence, serves to aid us
all in the maintenance of peace. It will become an effective
weapon in the war on poverty by opening the unbiased flood-
gates of economic promise and opportunity.

Promoting fairness without promoting reasonable rules
of peace has resulted in misunderstandings and obstacles to a
healthy humanity. Its cost has been calculated in lost opportunities in education and employment, corruption and crime,
a reduction in health brought on by stress, class warfare, disobedience to natural law, and a host of other tangible and
intangible cost. The most costly unfairness comes to those
who feel the world is passing them by, advancing without
them.

The development of Affirmative Action laws in the United
States are the result of painstaking thought into how this
nation must deal with its sins of the past and the consequences levied on today and the future. In 1963, the Reverend Dr. Martin Luther King, Jr., winner of the 1964 Nobel
Prize for Peace authored a book titled, *Why We Can't Wait*.

In his book Dr. King wrote:

Among those many vital jobs to be done, the nation must not only radically readjust its attitude toward the Negro in the compelling present, but must in its planning some compensatory consideration for the handicaps he has inherited from the past. It is impossible to create a formula for the future which does not take into account that our society has been doing something special against the Negro for hundreds of years. How then can he be absorbed into the mainstream of American life if we do not do something special for him now, in order to balance the equation and equip him to compete on a just and equal basis?

He continued:

Whenever this issue of compensatory of preferential treatment for the Negro is raised, some of our friends recoil in horror. The Negro should be granted equality, they agree; but he should ask nothing more. On the surface, this appears reasonable, but it is not realistic. For it is obvious that if a man is entered at the starting line in a race three hundred years after another man, the first would have to perform some impossible feat in order to catch up with his fellow runner.

These views are not accepted by most who consider themselves conservative today. Because this view is met with hostility in the absence of laws of peace, it has caused many hurt feelings and has resurrected many ghosts of prejudice. Replace the word *Negro* with *Native American, Hispanic, Latino, Disabled, Gay,* or any other broad-basing term depicting the special form of prejudice and bigotry exhibited in our society. Replace the *he's* used by Dr. King with *she's*. Stand these new participants on the scene and apply such words as glass ceiling, discrimination, classism, and a host of other descriptives, and you have a formula that requires some sort of Affirmative Action policy.

It is true that the backlash of such policies wrongfully punishes many individuals seeking opportunity, but it serves to heal wounds of a society of individuals injured by the willful acts of violence against and handicapping of groups of people pregnant with promise. Recently, many misinformed persons have given voice to the injustice of Affirmative Action plans. But, how many persons opposing Affirmative Action have come forward with plans to alleviate the scars of past wounds. Past wrongs that have left groups of individuals, especially African Americans and women, disadvantaged by an Affirmative Active policy that rewards individuals on the basis of their European-male gift of birth alone? How many noticed the rewards of guarded parity issued only to those who willfully adjust and assimilate themselves to be accepted by the culture reserving economic and political power to itself?

One of the many problems with Affirmative Action is that it has been applied faultily in the absence of constructive means aligned with the laws of peace. It has allowed evil men to hire tokens and persons unqualified to hold various positions to instigate a ground-swell of support opposing Affirmative Action. Add to this formula, an ignorance of history and an intolerance for people who are different and you have created a dangerously volatile force charged to destroy any gains on the development of peace.

Affirmative Action is just one of many glaring examples of hotly debated politically-charged bits of rhetoric which challenges the development of peace in America. Crime, poverty, welfare, health care, and education are some of many issues when mixed with ignorance and seasoned with hatred that makes for an antagonizing ill will in the development of peace.

We have stood by the current climate of hostility and hatred long enough. The peace movement has stagnated and lays hopelessly near death. It must be revived. It calls for the active support of every man, woman, boy, and girl. In the darkness of terrorism and rise of hate groups at an alarming rate, we must make a dash for the light of hope. This light is the illumination of people working together for peace.

The Nation's Prologue

Throughout history, the continuous story of conflict is told. From the dawn of mankind are the stories of battles resulting from the confrontations of superior and inferior beings. By superficial measures of possessions, physical appearance, geopolitical, and religious alignments, we have learned, as humans, to look down on and berate others who do not mirror our own status. Likewise, we have learned to hold high those who display what we hope to be. Movie stars, sports heroes, politicians, ministers of all backgrounds are just a few of the many mega-people we tend to hold up daily as figures we wish to exemplify. This mood defeats the first and second laws in the *Ten Commandments of Peace:*

1. Know and Respect Yourself;
2. Know and Respect Others.

When we all begin to believe we are somebody, then we will begin the process toward peace. We are able to participate in and contribute to the fabric of humanity, restoring beauty to the design chosen by its Creator. Those ignorant but brave souls who set sail several centuries ago were explorers ignorant of geography but strong in courage. Their wandering leadership opened the doors, for scores of explorers to follow. The non-explorers were the oppressed seekers of freedom. Some of those non-explorers sought religious liberty, others sought political independence, yet others sought a place to go. The ships transporting the immigrants saw the opportunity to greatly expand into this vast wonderland of good fortune. Many were over-excited. They were so over-excited that they made evil voyages onto another continent to transport people, by force, to share by their labor in the building of a nation. Slavery, known to every group from every period of civilized man, was a project gone wrong by the forces of greed and wealth. It placed into the psyche of a nation a peculiar and evil concept based on an untested premise that one group of individuals were superior and the other inferior, based on the color of skin alone. It depresses the theory that nature selectively has washed humanity with genius and insanity. Failure to understand this, defeats the third and fourth law in the *Ten Commandments of Peace:*

3. Respect the laws of nature;

4. Appreciate the mutual design of humanity.

However the means, a ship sailed by voyagers seeking opportunity or a ship piloted by a hostile force denying the opportunities they seek, the ships have landed. We all, by Divine Providence are citizens of the City of Hope, the United States of America. Some of our progenitors were more responsible for the infrastructure of this nation while others were more responsible for the creeds and laws established to govern this nation. Those who fail to understand this defeat the fifth law in the *Ten Commandments of Peace:*

5. Appreciate the Accomplishments and Intelligence of Others.

We all have forbearers who aided in the building of our nation. Present before us is the choice to continue in its construction.

From the sower of seed to the scouter of space, that surveys the stretch of our universe, are the many genderless. raceless, ageless, unaligned and non-partisan persons whose wonder promotes the growth and reach of a people. During the twentieth century, we have advanced from trotting along on horseback to flying in planes only surpassed in velocity by the movement of information by electronic means. Those who deny the active participation of all humanity sell themselves short and defeat the sixth law in the Ten Commandments of Peace:

6. *Be honest, never patronizing.*

We are patronizing when we assume we are in agreement with this law, but find ourselves categorizing people into some caste system of lots drawn up by the individual at will.

Many of us are so used to this human-designed caste system, that we see others through a vision distorted by the outward appearance of humanity. We know of every group of people classed by some superficial element of kinship. We close the windows of individuality, shut the doors of greater opportunity, and slow the advancement of civilization. We have become techno-beasts. We are surrounded and supported by things. We are losing our humanity. We habitually defeat the seventh law in the *Ten Commandments of Peace:*

7. Avoid Blanket Statements.

Until now we have broken so many rules that from many directions, we attempt to repair the disaster that has given rise to prejudices, bigotries, and other diseases eating at our world. I truly believe most people are of goodwill and desire peace. Mothers and fathers desire safety for themselves and their children. Children would prefer to grow in a world unencumbered by threats of violence and annihilation. Most who consider this have ideas and methods by which to achieve these noble desires and preferences. Our unwillingness to examine these theories to achieve peace have resulted in the establishment of war. This becomes a direct result of our disobedience to the eighth law in the *Ten Commandments of Peace:*

8. Respect the right to dissent.

At times, our intent and determination to be right have been so keen that it lacks honest review of its impact and has become a movement of wrong instead. Then, to make matters worse, we have attempted to maintain our social status maintaining our wrongful position at the expense of the innocent. In my nation, it is usually not a showing of pride and strength to acknowledge and atone for our wrong doing. This has kept on edge, many years past slavery and even the Civil Rights Act of 1965, the volatile relationship between the descendants from the continents of Europe and Africa. It also defies the ninth law in the *Ten Commandments of Peace:*

9. Always be willing to apologize and ready to forgive.

Our nation's history is so filled with the personal and institutional transgressions of these natural laws that it has become impossible to maintain a healthy respect. The lack of respect draws a limit to the prospects for a lasting peace. In doing so we have limited our example and betrayed our voice of unity to the world. We are hyper and alert as a nation and ready to do battle. Spend is the battle cry of politicians as unsubstantiated funding is poured into its military machine.

Charge against the future is the cry of foolish leaders lacking responsibility of the nation's economy to maintain our fighting forces. We are at full alert and must be, if we are to maintain a strong defense and power for peace throughout the world. Yet, we must be very watchful but, able to rest and give peace a chance. If we fail to, we break even the simplest law in the *Ten Commandments of Peace:*

10. Take Time to Rest.

Most Americans have a working knowledge of history and the events we hold sacred in the establishment of our nation. However, most of us fail in our understanding of American history and the implications of the past to the present. Every social conflict that we face today is rooted in our blood-stained history and failure to honor these natural laws of peace. Thankfully, it is not too late to begin obeying them.

We must learn these laws. We must live with these laws in constant use. We must share these laws from the moment that our children begin to talk. We must instill them in our nation's character by teaching them in our schools, our churches, our communities, and organizations. Those who protect our peace, our armed forces and state, county and municipal police officers, must apply them. Our judges must live by them. Our political leaders must promote them. From every foreseeable angle, we must practice the Ten Commandments of Peace.

In the late 1950s and early 1960s, a new leader emerged. This leader was an embattled soldier of peace. His weapons were truth and justice as he mounted a campaign against the soul of a nation as defined by its creed and laws. This leader enlisted the support of many crossing the invisible barriers of race. They came running, young and old, assigning themselves responsibility in a war of peace. Male and female locked arms in unity and song as they sang, "We Shall Overcome."

Their leader and drum major was inspired by a dream of what we could be. He understood the documents of America's conscience and led a nation to request of its leaders the pouring out of its rights and privileges to all of its citizens regardless of their differences. He sounded the challenges of the Declaration of Independence and the Constitution. His assault was not as much to gain ground for himself, as for the generations to come. The Reverend Dr. Martin Luther King, Jr. flanked by the officers Ralph Abernathy, Asa Philip Randolph, Andrew Young, Jr., James Farmer, John Lewis, Roy Wilkins, Hosea Williams, and Jesse Jackson, were with many others like Rev. Fred Shuttlesworth and Medgar Evers, begging this nation to share its rights of positive and natural law. They were faced by hoses, dogs, fire, and even bullets, but they still pressed on.

In 1963, Dr. King published his reasoning for the eagerness of want for all Americans to share in America's promise. The book was titled, *Why We Can't Wait*. At that time King was a mere prince, not yet king of civil rights and civil justice. By motivating Americans, he caused them to reach beyond their limitations and overcome prejudice, hate and intolerance. With a throng of persons tired and weary of the status quo, he marched to the throne. Upon this throne he challenged the sovereignty of the nation's documents and its design for governance. Dr. King promoted the intelligent of our nation to wonder: *could the U.S. Declaration of Independence, that legally gave birth to a nation, stand the test of consistency and modern reasoning?*

What does it mean to hold a self-evident truth that all men are created equal and endowed by their creator with certain inalienable rights?

What does it mean whenever any form of government becomes destructive of these ends; it is the right of the people to alter or abolish it?

What does it mean to alter or institute a new government with its powers organized, in such form, as to most likely protect this "inalienable right" to "safety and happiness?"

King George, was replaced by a commonwealth of kings. These kings, like George, were also guilty. By the despotic authority and power, granted to a race of people on the basis of skin color and heritage alone, they allowed abuses and usurpations of rights granted to others by God. Worse than the tyrannical powers of one ruler was the tyranny of one group of people over another. With this understanding, Dr. King rose to establish a God-given power to peacefully declare war on a kingdom bent on hoarding justice and civil rights selfishly for those deemed racially worthy.

In the 1950s struggle for justice, the right to sit anywhere in a bus was wrestled out of its prejudiced grip. However this, as effective as it was, paled by comparison with the battle to come. In the face of America's legal authority, the U.S. Constitution, a blow of challenge was thrown. The nation had fallen. It wasn't knocked out; it was simply knocked down. Here, sense was pounded into the conscience of the national psyche. Breath by breath, citizens thought to be blessed with truth and liberty, were forced to consider the fairness of the game. In this ring, the oppressed, led by Dr. King, again tried to have wrongs redressed, only to be wronged again.

The hour was right. Once more in history, the time had come. It was time for a people, so oppressed by disrespect, fought by prejudice, killed by bigotry, and buried by hatred, to rise. Resurrection day had come. Those looking in the direction of the cemetery, resting bodies of truth, justice, civil rights, and civil liberties, witnessed the rise. Dr. King found the support of a multicultured army of soldiers. This army was made up of men and women, Jews and Gentiles, Protestants and Catholics, Muslins, Gays, Lesbians and scores of others enlisted in a war for peace. He witnessed the revival of life. Together they made movement toward a righteous throne established on justice. Step by step, the documents Americans cherish, were challenged. How valid were the opening words to the Constitution's preamble, "We the People?" Who were the people? What was a "more perfect union?" Was justice really established? Where was domestic tranquillity? While the citizens of this nation were defended from foreign attacks and intrusions, who saw to it that the population of home was defended against itself? With the standard of the living being held in check by contempt and a socio-economic embargo of opportunity to the human descendant of slaves, who was the "general welfare" promoted for? Who were the Americans and generations of Americans to come who would find the blessings of liberty?

Was it the 1865 Emancipation Proclamation that ended slavery in America? No! This document only served to abolish slavery in states and territories then in rebellion to the union. It was not until some months later that the ratification and signing into law of the 13th Amendment to the U.S. Constitution:

> Neither slavery nor involuntary servitude except as a punishment for crime . . . shall exist within the United States, or any place subject to their jurisdiction.

This ended the evil of human enslavement.

Three years after the legal end of slavery, the fourteenth amendment was signed into the same document of granted rights. This amendment was the guarantee of citizen rights afforded any persons born, or naturalized in the U.S. Here "no state" is allowed to

> make or enforce any law which shall abridge the privileges of immunities of citizens of the United States; nor shall any state deprive any person of life, liberty, or property without due process of law; nor, deny any person within its jurisdiction the equal protection of the law.

Two years later, in 1872, the voting rights of African Americans and all citizens was signed into America's law. Having been granted citizenship and citizen rights by the former law, the fifteenth amendment served to extend, by law and regardless of race, color, or previous condition of servitude, the undeniable and unabridged right of American men to elect leaders by ballot. Surprisingly, not until some 50 years later, in 1920, were the same rights granted to women in the 19th amendment. Even more amazing, a year after the publication of Dr. King's book, the federal government of the United States of America saw the need to establish the twenty fourth amendment. This amendment to the constitution prohibited a poll tax.

In order to subvert the reach of America's supreme positive law, which grants us civil rights and liberties, wicked men devised ill-intended laws no different than the Jim Crow enforcements of the past. State after state, especially in the Bible belt, drafted legislation and passed laws which required the disenfranchising of those unable to pay a poll tax. This reach of law pushed, picked, and promoted as a way to handle civil unrest, brought on by exclusion. It was the result of prejudiced and bigoted men, hostile to the efforts of peace. Thankfully, the misguided reach of ill will was cut off, era by era, by strong persons of goodwill and intelligence.

Today with the rise of an inhumane form of conservatism and a fascist-style nationalism pulling us back to an unkind era of American history, we are called to reach for the rights granted by our unique documents of national creed and law. We are called to guard the fortress against the polished and practiced politicians, wickedly beguiling the American citizen. They preach peace as they explode with hate and contempt, for those they deem undeserving of America's promise. Those not represented by the newly-emerging power in America are those who were traditionally held back at the start of the race, wrongly positioned to run the race and teased by the goal which offers equal opportunity to all participants. These are the men and women who act with a sense of false superiority.

The challenges noted by Dr. King in 1963, were relative to race. He enlisted the aid of all persons of goodwill to rise up and lock arms in brother-and sisterhood. By a groundswell of support, a campaign for peace was launched. Together they call for justice. Peace will not, because it can not, exist where justice is denied. Peace is replaced by hostility and distress when hope is overshadowed. Peace falls from the equation which variables present bigotry, hatred, prejudice, chauvinism, ill will, and contempt. Peace fades into false images of political security as leaders devour the disadvantaged, walk on the wounded, harass the hard-pressed, trash the troubled, and ignore the injured. It was Benedict De Spinoza who in his *Theological-Political Treatise* wrote: "Peace is not an absence of war, it is a virtue, a state of mind, a disposition for benevolence, confidence, justice."

In 1963, the fight was focused on the African-American community. That fight was a victorious battle but not the end of the war. It did, however, facilitate a forced right to be spoken from the ballot box. It caused many Americans to see and reckon with injustice. That fight fanned the flames of torches, lighting the way out of a dark era of U.S. history. It forced open doors of opportunity in education, employment, housing, public accommodations, access to the courts, and rights to due process. Refuge in the family of American opportunity found rest.

The non-violent soldiers of the late '50s and early '60s were met by violent men. Together they battled over reach of civil liberties and rights. Together they appealed to a high judge who deemed Natural Law greater than "Man-made Law." This decision has given African-Americans new hope and opportunity.

As we move into the 21st Century, I invite you, the reader, to join with me in a new battle. This new battle is similar to the old battle. It calls for respect to all and human rights for all. It calls for tolerance above difference. It calls for a cease fire by the atomic arsenal of bigotry, chauvinism, and prejudice. I invite you all to aid me in the demolition of the invisible walls that divide us. Join with me and fight for the rights of liberty and justice. During these few years left before entering the new era, I am begging you to work for peace. Let your work represent care. Continue to care until the sound of real freedom is unmuffled and allowed to ring from every mountainside. As long as a person can sign up to defend his or her nation, but due to the color of his or her skin, is denied justice presented with harassment by officials sworn to uphold law, we must fight. As long as women represent the armed forces abroad but are shielded by a glass ceiling at home, we must fight. As long as immigration is open to all people, but seen as a threat from America's southern border. As long as laws are passed to dishonor native tongues and immigrant children denied the rights spelled out in the 14th amendment, we must fight.

We must fight to lift the stigma of the inner city and restore hope. Political rhetoric has judiciously, in many ways, replaced the term "nigger" with "inner city" and anyone living there is associated with drugs, prostitution, rape, theft, welfare, and murder. The so-called inner city is broadbrushed as a chaotic zoo of beasts who roam freely under clouds of disaster. This stereotype portraying the inner city is also seen in suburbia, whose homes are shaded by trees and places of residence divided by paths of green. The problems of the inner city are American problems. For too long these problems have stood in the way of progress and opportunity. For those blind to hope, we must fight.

As long as those challenged by impaired hearing and speech impediments, or other physical limitations, brought on naturally, or by accident, are regarded as less than human in hiring and accommodations, we must fight. As long as lesbians and gays are regarded as less than human and denied housing, jobs, and the rights legally afforded to heterosexuals, we must fight. This charge, at the end of the 20th century, is a call for fairness and justice. Without these, it is difficult to sustain peace.

The *Ten Commandments of Peace* do not require legislation. No judicial precedent, executive order, or new bureaucracy needs to be established. It does not require paying more in taxes. If anything, it should aid in the reduction of taxes by lowering the cost of government by crime, conflict, and war. It helps the educator to teach in a non-confrontational, noncombative atmosphere and leads to a more efficient use of time. It invites the parents and guardians of children to train the child to see others undistorted by the physical nature. It allows churches to promote diversity especially in the Christian community where Christ preached and practiced the same. Choosing to live by these simple laws is a choice to respect all, regardless of their differences and superficial nature. To this we cannot wait.

To move the world along, I must begin at home. I would like with your help and support, to sign by the year 2000, more than 150 million Americans to a treaty of peace. This treaty of peace is no more than an agreement to try daily to live by the *Ten Commandments of Peace*. With the serious efforts of all we can:

- Remove walls of prejudice;
- Open greater opportunity to all;
- Create greater responsibility;
- Promote the promise of democracy;
- Chose our children over chaos;
- Allow intelligent reasoning over ignorant reaction;
- Promote positive activity or prevent negative action;
- Promote wisdom over weapons; and
- Create communication over confrontation; and
- promote peace over power.

Real peace is power. This power is love. Love is of God. Today is the day to choose peace and, to these ends, we must keep moving. Before we reach the year 2000, this maybe your *One Last Call*. God bless you.

We welcome comments from our readers. Feel free to write to us at the following address:

Editorial Department
Prescott Press
P.O. Box 53788
Lafayette, LA 70505

More Good Books

Alzheimer's:
Making Sense of Suffering
by Teresa R. Strecker, Ph.D.

Alzheimer's's: Making Sense of Suffering was written for the caregivers and loved ones of Alzheimer's victims, providing them spiritual guidance and support. The author shares her own journey while watching a loved one suffer with Alzheimer's.

ISBN 1-56384-133-9

Getting Out:
An Escape Manual for Abused Women
by Kathy L. Cawthon

Four million women are physically assaulted by their husbands, ex-husbands, and boyfriends each year. Of these millions of women, nearly 4,000 die. Kathy Cawthon, herself a former victim of abuse, uses her own experience and the expertise of law enforcement personnel to guide the reader through the process of escaping an abusive relationship. *Getting Out* also shows readers how they can become whole and healthy individuals instead of victims, giving them hope for a better life in the future.

ISBN: 1-56384-093-6

Journey into Darkness: Nowhere to Land
by Stephen L. Arrington

This story begins on Hawaii's glistening sands and ends in the mysterious deep with the Great White Shark. In between, he found himself trapped in the drug smuggling trade—unwittingly becoming the "Fall Guy" in the highly publicized John Z. DeLorean drug case. Naval career shattered, his youthful innocence tested, and friends and family put to the test of loyalty, Arrington locked on one truth during his savage stay in prison and endeavors to share that critical truth now. Focusing on an important message to young people—to stay away from drugs—the author recounts his horrifying prison experience and allows the reader to take a peek at the source of hope and courage that helped him survive.

ISBN 1-56384-003-3

High on Adventure: Stories of Good, Clean, Spline-tingling Fun
High on Adventure II: Dreams Becoming Reality
High on Adventure III: Building the Dream Machine
by Stephen L. Arrington

Author and adventurer Stephen Arrington tells many exciting tales from his life as a navy frogman and chief diver and expedition leader for The Cousteau Society, lacing each story with his Christian belief and outlook that life is an adventure waiting to be had. In the *High on Adventure* Series, you'll meet a seventeen-and-a-half-foot Great White shark face-to-face, dive from an airplane toward the earth's surface at 140 M.P.H., explore a sunken battle cruiser from World War II in the dark depths of the South Pacific Ocean, explore molten lava as it flows underwater, climb earth's newest volcano and many other exciting tales. "Each of us is standing on a threshold where the future will be determined by our daily choices and commitment to excellence," says Arrington. With the right habits and motivation, a mundane life can explode into a challenging, adventure-filled quest full of opportunity, fun, and happiness. Arrington shows people, young and old, that dreams can become a reality.

High on Adventure I   ISBN 1-56384-082-0
High on Adventure II   ISBN 1-56384-115-0
High on Adventure III   ISBN 1-56384-144-4

The Unicorn Whisperer

Another Phoebe and Her Unicorn Adventure

Dana Simpson

Andrews McMeel
PUBLISHING®

Complete Your Phoebe and Her Unicorn Collection

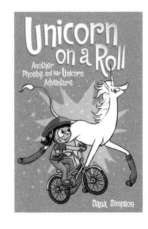

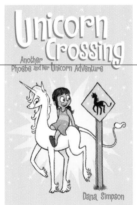

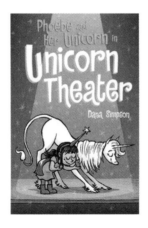

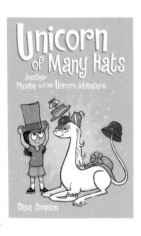

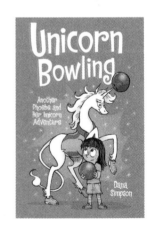

Hey, kids!

Check out the glossary starting on page 172
if you come across words you don't know.

On the first day of school, it's always really hard to focus.

Could you cast some sort of... *focus spell* on me?

I could...

But I must warn you, a focus spell is difficult to calibrate, so it carries certain risks.

Could you repeat that? I got distracted by that pine-cone.

I shall prepare the spell.

How did the concentration spell work out for you?

The results were really mixed.

I kept getting stuck concentrating on random things, but I also got a week's worth of home-work done in class, so my afternoons are free for a while.

dana

Also...I think my freckles might be turning rainbow-colored.

A temporary side effect, but a stylish one.

21

Once upon a time, there was a girl named...

Phoebina.

Phoebina. And her parents were the king and queen of a magical far-off land!

King Ethan and Queen Emily were very proud of the princess, whose best friend was a unicorn.

DOUBLE unicorn.

However, King Ethan thought the princess got greedy at times.

King Ethan and Queen Emily were very proud of Princess Phoebina.

They were her parents. Parents have to be.

It wasn't just that.

She was smart. And weird. And way better than the king at Ultra Go-Kart Racing 8.

He wasn't just letting her win?

That wouldn't have been very kingly of him.

We unicorns got the idea for Pohúmon Go from you humans, of course.

If *YOU* can enjoy pretending to catch magical creatures, we can pretend to capture you back.

Of course, my "Phoebe" remains the jewel of my collection.

Aw, you're sweet. And thanks for not trapping me inside a ball.

dana

31

Maybe you wouldn't have to stare at your reflection if you were LESS PRETTY.

What if you made a really weird face every time you saw your reflection?

AAA NOT WORTH IT.

Sometimes the cure is worse than the disease.

42

Unicorns invented jumping rope, you know.

Once, long ago, a unicorn named *Chrysanthemum Goldenflanks* was fond of constantly jumping in place, and everyone made fun of her.

So she incorporated a bit of rope, and soon it was all the rage!

I'd jump up and down a lot more MYSELF if it were socially acceptable.

We all would.

Next time, I DON'T think I'll have you enchant my bubble wand.

I used to ride the school bus
(It was crowded, as a rule)

But that was then, and now I ride
A unicorn to school!

Sometimes I used to miss the bus
My mom would get irate

But now however long I take
My unicorn will wait.

I saw the world through windows
That were high above the ground

But now I see and hear and smell
The beauty all around.

I still could ride the school bus
(It's one way to get to school)

But take my word that unicorns
Are way way WAY more cool.

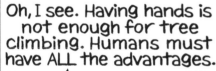

What should we do for Halloween costumes this year?

We could go as NOTHING. I could render us invisible!

How would anyone know to give us candy, then?

They would not, but nor would they notice if we TOOK the candy.

I think hanging out with humans is making you devious.

When I said your species had nothing to teach mine, I was SO WRONG.

Hey Dad. I have SUPER-POWERS now, thanks to Marigold!

Really? What kind?

Well...

So far, I can levitate a couple feet off the ground, and wash dishes by looking at them.

Sometimes bragging has a heavy price.

An important lesson for a young superhero.

Marigold gave me actual superpowers as part of my Halloween costume!

Whoa, cool!

Do you need a sidekick?

Sure, if you're offering!

I asked Marigold, but she doesn't DO "sidekick." For some reason she'd rather be my *arch-nemesis*.

dana

FEAR THE WRATH OF POINTYHEAD.

It's a side of her you don't usually see.

89

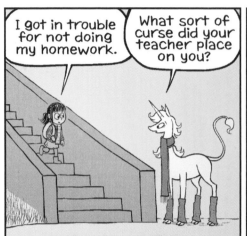

The actual Tooth Fairy is rather unlike the legend.

She does collect teeth, but she is discerning! Her interest is only in unique, special teeth!

She pays handsomely for teeth she finds worthy of the *Tooth Fairy Dental Museum*

Oo, let's go there!

It is small. I would have to shrink us. And the cafeteria is only so-so.

99

knock
knock

Marigold!

I am down to 15% magnificence.

Can I help?

I smell cocoa. The sparkly marshmallows will restore my strength.

It has come to the attention of the Unicorn High Council that you have EXCEEDED your allotment of magic for this day.

This is just a friendly warning. Have a sparkling day, Marigold Heavenly Nostrils!

You used up MORE magic with Stephanie than you EVER have with me!

In a single day, but you are way ahead, all-time.

That just means she has a higher average score than me.

113

115

116

This next aria is the centerpiece of the opera. It celebrates the Goddess of Renewal.

Wait, that's—

Dakota?!

I did wonder how we got such excellent seats!

I wanna be in a goblin opera.

The other kids in my group project asked me to go to the library during recess to work on it.

Did you go?

Of course not. Why waste my recess?

It's due in two days, so I figure I'll just do the whole thing tomorrow night.

Why not now?

I'm not just working for three, I'm PROCRASTINATING for three.

Quick! Everybody get out your communicators!

Look at that. Their "communicators" are five times the size of my phone!

And why does the computer on their ship make all those "beep boop beep" noises? Computers don't make that sound.

dana

Because the actual future is disappointing.

I really wouldn't know.

How come you never wear a helmet when you rollerskate?

I am wearing an *INVISIBLE* helmet! It is enchanted so as to let my mane blow freely, but still protect my head.

Unfortunately, they are not available in human sizes, as yet.

They never make the best stuff in human sizes.

Well, I envy your ease in finding fitting pants.

Dakota got her ears pierced. She thinks that's yet another way she's cooler than me.

Is she?

Psh. No.

Good, because I would hate to imagine I have been spending so much time with a LESS THAN OPTIMALLY COOL child!

You're being sarcastic.

I am soooo glad you have finally learned to tell.

dana

On partly cloudy nights like this, when some of the stars are concealed...

...the regular constellations are ruined, but it is an opportunity to invent NEW ones.

That cluster of stars is normally part of the constellation *Steve the Unicorn*, but partly obscured, it looks more like...um...

Cynthia the unicorn?

Yes! Who has much shorter legs than Steve.

WHOA!

What is that STRANGE GLOWING OBJECT in the sky? I can't recall EVER seeing it before! It must be a UFO!

We surrender, alien overlords! Just don't HURT us!

Dad makes this joke on EVERY sunny winter day.

Take the girl and the unicorn if you must! Just spare me!

153

Oh dear...Dakota is watching Phoebe with a derisive smirk.

I must help her! I shall *enchant her kickboard!*

AAAAAAAAAAAAAAAAAAAAA

"And there I beheld the most remarkable of unicorn confections:"

"A *SUGAR DODECAHEDRON.* Twelve sides of pure sugary goodness."

You know what else has twelve sides? *TWO CUBES.*

Yes, but that is less fun to say.

AUGHPTHB!

What is wrong?

I WALKED INTO A SPIDERWEB!

So you are feeling pangs of guilt for having destroyed the spider's hard work?

YES ACTUALLY BUT IT'S NOT MY MAIN CONCERN!

Why do spiders bother you so much?

I dunno...it's creepy how they have eight legs!

As a little filly, I knew a UNICORN who had eight legs! Her name was Annabelle.

Although...now that I think about it, Anna and Belle MAY have been two separate unicorns who frequently stood next to each other.

It is funny realizing one still carries childhood misconceptions.

I forget what I was freaked out by, so thanks I guess.

GLOSSARY

aesthetically (es-thet-ick-lee): pg. 93 – adverb / in a way that is visually appealing and provides enjoyment and satisfaction through beauty

arpeggio (arr-pej-ee-oh): pg. 11 – noun / the notes of a chord played in order, either ascending up the scale, or descending back down the scale

befuddlement (bee-fudd-uhl-ment): pg. 58 – noun / confusion

berobed (bi-row-bd): pg. 130 – adjective / wearing a robe

capitalism (kah-pi-tuh-lizm): pg. 100 – noun / an economic system in which trade and commerce are controlled by private owners for profit

compromise (kom-pro-mize): pg. 9 – noun / an agreement when two sides "meet in the middle" by giving up some demands in order to still get something that they both want

constellation (kon-stuh-lay-shun): pg. 144 – noun / a cluster of stars that can be linked together to form an imaginary outline or picture (such as the Big Dipper)

extraterrestrial (ek-struh-tuh-res-tree-ul): pg. 5 – adjective / something that is from beyond the Earth and outside its atmosphere

indigestion (in-duh-jest-shun): pg. 147 – noun / the feeling of an upset stomach or discomfort in the upper abdomen, usually caused by diet

karma (car-muh): pg. 89 – noun / the belief that your actions help cause what you experience in the future, or the idea that "what goes around, comes around"

levitate (lev-i-tayt): pg. 70 – verb / to float several feet above the ground

luxuriate (lucks-shur-ee-ayt): pg. 59 – verb / to relax in fancy surroundings, or by consuming fine food and drink

metaphorical (me-tuh-for-i-kuhl): pg. 7 – adjective / relating to a figure of speech in which words are used to make a comparison between two things that are different but have something in common

meteorites (mee-tee-or-ites): pg. 102 – noun / a solid piece of debris from a comet, asteroid, or meteoroid that travels through outer space and the atmosphere to reach the surface of a planet or moon

mollified (mol-lih-fyd): pg. 26 – verb (past participle) / soothed or made calm after being angry

platonic (pluh-ton-ick): pg. 158 – adjective / an affectionate relationship that is friendly in nature rather than romantic

primate (pry-mayt): pg. 158 – noun / an order of mammal including monkeys, apes, and humans

procrastinating (pro-krass-ti-nate-ing): pg. 134 – verb / delaying or putting off until a later time what could be done today

subtle (suh-tuhl): pg. 139 – adjective / understated, muted, or low-key

whitecaps (whyt-kaps): pg. 46 – noun / the part of small waves that form a white foamy top (or "crest") in windy or stormy conditions

Andrews McMeel Publishing
a division of Andrews McMeel Universal
1130 Walnut Street, Kansas City, Missouri 64106

www.andrewsmcmeel.com

19 20 21 22 23 RR2 10 9 8 7 6 5 4 3 2

ISBN: 978-1-5248-5196-5

Library of Congress Control Number: 2019932740

Made by:
LSC Communications US, LLC
Address and location of manufacturer:
1009 Sloan Street
Crawfordsville, IN 47933
2nd Printing—10/25/19

ATTENTION: SCHOOLS AND BUSINESSES

Andrews McMeel books are available at quantity discounts with bulk purchase for educational, business, or sales promotional use. For information, please e-mail the Andrews McMeel Publishing Special Sales Department: specialsales@amuniversal.com.

Look for these books!

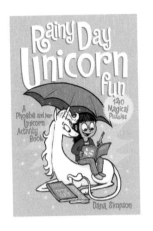

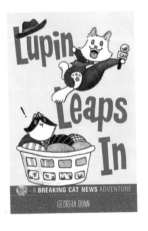